Lost in Translation

Lost in Translation

Rediscovering the
Hebrew Roots of Our Faith

John Klein & Adam Spears
with Michael Christopher

Lost in Translation: Rediscovering the Hebrew Roots of Our Faith
(Previously published as *Devils and Demons and the Return of the Nephilim*)

Covenant Research Institute
PO Box 8224
Bend, OR 97708
www.lostintranslation.org

Publishing services by Selah Publishing Group, LLC, Tennesee. The views expressed or implied in this work do not necessarily reflect those of Selah Publishing Group.

ISBN: 978-1-58930-199-3
Library of Congress Control Number: 2007905767

Contents

Foreword

When I was a young man I had a hard time learning to shave. Didn't matter how much lather or how sharp the blade. If I'd been standing with my toes in the ocean the sharks would have beached themselves trying to get at me. As it was, I grew up many miles from the coast but my sink still had bite marks around the edges.

I specifically remember going to my busboy job in a local restaurant with thirteen fresh cuts on my face. I can't remember what my boss said when he saw me. By the time he stopped laughing I was in no mood to hear it anyway. But I do know what eventually happened.

My skin toughened up and I stopped whacking myself every time I shaved. In due course I even developed enough assurance to cut against the grain, dragging the razor uphill for a closer trim.

In a sense, maybe that's a major theme of this book. In the last two decades, so much of what God has shown to John Klein and Adam Spears has drawn them thousands of years backwards, into the ancient biblical past. They have not gone against the grain of common sense, but once or twice they have certainly scraped against the grain of conventional thought.

To some extent that might be what attracted me and my wife, Patricia, to classes taught by these two minister/teachers in the first place. We have now worked with them through countless hours on the present book, debriefing, organizing, and helping them verify from scriptural and historical sources the material it contains. But never once have we lost that spark that first drew us to this project, that overarching, ever-present, always-poignant awareness that God often speaks through persons unknown outside their own households.

More to the point, John Klein and Adam Spears are uniquely willing to still their own voices and let God do the talking. It is our joint hope that He will be heard throughout every chapter in this book, urging us to look to Him alone, via the ancient history of His chosen people, for answers to questions many students of His Word seem to ask of other sources instead.

In that regard the two authors devote plenty of space in the pages ahead to demonstrating that the Bible is an ancient Hebrew book from cover to cover, reflecting ancient Hebrew customs, culture, and idiomatic understandings. Recent discoveries, most notably the Dead Sea Scrolls, strongly suggest that at least 90 percent of it came down to us originally in the ancient Hebrew language. When we consider all these factors together, the Bible becomes even more profound, consistent, and remarkable than most of us have been taught.

The God who gave us Genesis is the same God who gave us Revelation, unchanged and unchanging, still filled with the same love for us that he poured out upon Adam, Ruth, John, Mary, and his own Son. He is also the same God who made a clear distinction between devils, nephilim, and demons, listed in this sentence in what we might call "birthing" order.

This brings up three final points that we need to cover before we begin. First, the devils/nephilim/demons connection is not the only "unconventional" concept explored within these pages. And it's probably not even the most significant. It's very hard to understand the Bible if you don't understand biblical covenant, and it's next-to-impossible when you get to Revelation. This book will show you why.

Second, as the chapters ahead will make clear, this book is volume one of a multivolume *Lost in Translation* series. There's more to come, building on the foundation laid down in the pages ahead.

Finally, this book was not written by one person alone, but John Klein was probably the first guy in the door. Therefore, in the early pages of this first volume, John is the "I" who will sometimes peek over the top of the words.

But John Klein and Adam Spears began studying together as a team a long time before they began this book. Indeed, when they teach as a team it's not the least bit uncommon to find them finishing sentences for each other and amplifying each other's thoughts.

Basically, they've done the same kind of thing throughout this book. Because, for each of these two men, understanding more about the Hebraic background of the Scriptures has been almost a lifelong obsession, yet neither one ever seems to cover his ears or close his mind. To a remarkable degree, these volumes – especially the one that will follow soon, focusing on the book of Revelation – illustrate how much God is eager to teach us if we really mean it when we ask Him for more understanding.

He is the source and we are the vessels.

Michael Christopher
Bend, Oregon
September, 2007

1

Scriptural Foundations

It is the glory of God to conceal a matter,
but the glory of kings is to search out a matter.
Proverbs 25:2

Since I was fifteen years old I have been a student of the Bible. I have read and reread it, over and over. I sometimes find this part hard to believe, but that now amounts to more than thirty-five years of intensive study.

I have been especially intrigued by the prophetic books: Daniel, Isaiah, Jeremiah, Joel, Ezekiel, Amos, Revelation, and the others. I've read them all, multiple times, in every translation available, laboriously tracing references back and forth, reading every commentary I could get my hands on, searching for understanding.

I don't think I realized that I'd hit a dead end until one day, about seven years ago, when my frustration boiled over. I was driving down the road and I suddenly began to speak directly to God, partly in jest but also somewhat seriously.

"You know, God, I don't seem to get much in the way of 'new stuff' out of reading the Bible anymore! It would really be great to find out that you've given us another book. I need more help!"

And then I shut up and drove on down the road. But the thought didn't go entirely away.

Later that same day I was in the church where I worked as one of the pastors. As I walked by the office next to mine, I overheard the phrase, "No, devils aren't demons." I stopped in my tracks, stuck my head in, and said, "What? Devils aren't demons?"

That was the beginning of a life-changing experience for me. The speaker was the rabbi of a Messianic congregation in Bend, Oregon, called *Beit Simchat Torah*. He was a natural teacher with a better memory than any elephant ever born; a man who never met a fact he didn't like.

As he began to explain what he meant about devils and demons, drawing on his formal training, his understanding of the Hebrew language, and years of solitary, word-by-word study of the Bible, I suddenly became aware that he was looking at the Holy Scriptures from a perspective entirely different from mine.

For my own part, I'd just realized that I didn't know enough to get much *more* from the Scriptures on my own. I kept reading the same chapters over and over without learning anything new – little bits and pieces, maybe, but nothing like what used to hit me right between the eyes when I read it the first few times. I yearned for that initial excitement.

From that day forward, in 1996, the rabbi and I began to study together one night a week, from seven o'clock until midnight and sometimes well into the wee hours. Both of us saw immediately that we each had something the other needed. I had years of familiarity with English-language paraphrases of the Scriptures, which is what all the familiar translations are. I also had a dogged, literal mind that required every kernel of truth to line up perfectly with every other kernel. And all this seemed to be enhanced by an ability to see connections between various passages and references that aren't always obvious at first glance.

Before long, as our study relationship evolved, the rabbi would periodically resurrect the emerging joke between us by saying, "God gave you a new book, didn't He?!"

And yes, he did . . . but of course, it was the same one.

Understanding the Mysteries

In a year or so, we were joined by the co-author of this book, Adam Spears, a Messianic Jewish rabbi-in-training who has since taken charge of his first congregation. Adam was also a student of Hebrew culture and was every bit as determined to *understand the mysteries of the Scriptures* as I was.

I'll save the devil-demon discussion that launched our tiny study group for chapter four. Right now I want to concentrate on the initial impact on my own understanding of the Hebraic approach we were taking to the Word of God.

My research partner, Rabbi Richardson, had gone back to the Bible's Hebrew roots and had spent years researching the Scriptures from that perspective. In addition to the Hebrew language itself, he had studied ancient Hebrew history, culture, and customs. As a result he was thoroughly familiar with the social, economic, and religious context in which the Bible was written. And all of this was precisely what I was missing.

Until that point, in complete innocence I had approached Scripture from the Babylonian-Roman-Greek perspective so typical of most modern Bible students, who often still adhere to a system called "Greek hermeneutics" (*hier* = system of; *minutiae* = details). We'll discuss this in greater depth in chapter six, but for now, understand just one or two things.

First, when the ancient Greek philosophers translated Hebrew writings, of both the Old and the New Testament, they believed that the text "worked" on one of two levels only, the *literal* or the *allegorical* – and never both at the same time. Have you ever heard someone say, "Oh – that passage should be taken 'spiritually,' not literally?" Comments like that reflect the Greek hermeneutics approach.

Second, because the Greek philosophers had developed their methods by working on mythological texts, they were crippled by their assumption that the Hebrew text would also, automatically, reflect 75% creative imagination and only 25% truth. That left a lot of room for them to interject their own biases.

By contrast, Hebrew hermeneutics (also discussed at greater length in chapter six) is a rigorous system of logic used for detailed interpretation of the Hebrew Scriptures. It recognizes that about 98 percent of those Scriptures operate on four levels simultaneously: (1) *p'shat* – direct, simple; (2) *remez* – hinting; (3) *darash* – commentary, comparison; and (4) *sod* – deep, hidden.[1] Hebrew hermeneutics also require the interpreter to agree to a moral standard of unbiased translation. Nothing can be added or subtracted; to the Hebrew mind, scripture is 100% true, exactly as written. The goal is to recognize and understand that truth, wherever the hunt might lead.

When I began to re-read the Scriptures with a clearer understanding of the ancient Hebrew roots from which they sprang, things began to jump out at me again. And at Adam too, whose own background had once been remarkably similar to mine. We were like steel and flint together, flashing against each other, striking sparks and starting fires.

We all knew the scriptures fairly well, but suddenly many loose ends began to wrap themselves together for us. The reason is simple but it seems to escape so many people. The Old Testament is entirely a Hebrew document! There's not an American, Greek, Roman, or European writer anywhere in the bunch. Every single one was a Hebrew, and each one was literally given the words he put down by the God he knew as ADONAI.

And even though many scholars will still tell you that the original language of the New Testament was Greek, the evidence is overwhelming that much (or even *most*) of it, too, was first written in Hebrew. Even the parts that probably were given to us originally in Greek[2] were written by Hebrew men, from their own distinctly non-Greek perspectives. The authors grew up as Hebrews and looked at the world through Hebrew eyes. Again, there's not a Greek in the bunch – even Luke, commonly cited as the "exception," had a Hebrew father and was raised in a Hebrew household. That makes him Hebrew from the Biblical perspective.

The Matthew Document

What most scholars now call the *Mattityahu Document* (i.e., the *Matthew Document*) containing Matthew, Mark, Luke, and Acts 1:1–15:35 was written on one scroll, in Hebrew. Later on these were broken out into separate scrolls. It's difficult to be as certain about the other New Testament books, but many signs also indicate that the original text of Revelation, if not written in Hebrew, might have been recorded first in Aramaic, an ancient dialect of Hebrew.

Beyond all that, "Revelation's 404 verses contain as many as 278 quotes, or allusions to, the Old Testament [Tanakh],[3] especially Psalms, Isaiah, Ezekiel, Daniel, and Zechariah."[4]

In other words, 68.2% of Revelation either *is* or *contains* Hebrew Scripture, and the rest probably *is* or *does* the same!

The authors' Hebraic roots are especially evident throughout the three synoptic gospels. Matthew, Mark, and Luke[5] all tell essentially the same story of Yeshua[6] and His life on Earth. But more than that, they all tell it in language that uses nearly identical sentence structure, idiomatic expressions, and other distinguishing linguistic features that are all decidedly Hebrew, not Greek.

Here's a passage from *Understanding the Difficult Words of Jesus*,[7] by David Bivin and Roy Blizzard, Jr., Ph.D., two highly respected researchers who have studied, lectured, and written for years on exactly this issue:

> Our reasons for writing this book are not only to show that the original biography of Jesus was communicated in the Hebrew language, but to show that the entire New Testament can only be understood from a Hebraic perspective.
>
> Most Christians are aware that the Old Testament was originally communicated in Hebrew, and that it is important to know Hebrew to understand

the Old Testament. What they do not recognize, however, is the importance of Hebrew in understanding the New Testament.

It should be emphasized that the Bible (both Old *and* New Testaments) is, in its entirety, highly Hebraic. In spite of the fact that portions of the New Testament were communicated in Greek, the background is thoroughly Hebrew. The writers are Hebrew, the culture is Hebrew, the religion is Hebrew, the traditions are Hebrew, and the concepts are Hebrew.

We tend to forget that the Old Testament comprises approximately 78 percent of the biblical text, and the New Testament only 22 percent. When we add the highly Hebraic portions of the New Testament (Matthew, Mark, Luke, and Acts 1:1–15:35,* approximately 43 percent of the New Testament) to the Old Testament, the percentage of biblical material originally written in Hebrew rises to 88 percent (or 87 percent if we omit the portions of Ezra and Daniel – less than 1 percent of the Old Testament – composed in Aramaic). Not more than 12 percent of the entire Bible was originally written in Greek. When we subtract from that 12 percent the 176 quotations from the Old Testament (14 Old Testament quotations in John and 162 from Acts 15:36 to the end of the New Testament), the percentage of the Bible originally composed in Hebrew rises to over 90 percent.

The assumption that the entire New Testament was originally communicated in Greek has led to a considerable amount of misunderstanding on the part of scholars and laypersons alike. Today, as a result of recent research, we know that the key to our understanding of this material is Hebrew. To this present day there has been in New Testament studies a disproportionate stress placed on the study of Greek and Hellenism. If any additional advances are to be made, especially in better understanding the words of Jesus, the concentration must shift to the study of Hebrew history and culture, and above all, the Hebrew language.

Editor's Note: The preceding quotation also contains the following footnote, keyed to the asterisk on the words "Matthew, Mark, Luke, and Acts 1:1–15:35": "The first 15 chapters of Acts show some of the same textual evidence as the Synoptic Gospels of being originally communicated in Hebrew. They deal with events in Jerusalem and are recounted in a Hebrew context. In Acts 15:36 there is a shift to Greek as Luke himself begins to describe Paul's missionary journeys."

Little girl, arise!

In the fifth chapter of Mark we find a dramatic example of what can only be called a "shift" into the Hebrew language, a shift that makes no sense if the original language actually *was* Greek. One of the rulers of the synagogue, a man named Jairus, asked Yeshua to heal his young daughter, who lay gravely ill in a house some distance away. A few moments later, word came that the girl had already died. But Yeshua went anyway, and verses 39–42 tell what happened when He arrived:

> And entering in, He said to them, "Why make a commotion and weep? The child has not died, but is asleep." They began laughing at Him. But putting them all out, He took along the child's father and mother and His own companions, and entered the room where the child was. Taking the child by the hand, He said to her, "Talitha kumi!" (which translated means, "Little girl, I say to you, get up!").

> Immediately the girl got up and began to walk, for
> she was twelve years old. And immediately they
> were completely astounded. (Mark 5:39–42)

A more accurate translation of this idiomatic Hebrew expression, "Talitha kumi," would be, "Little girl in the talit, arise." The word *talit* refers to the prayer shawl that ancient Hebrew men and women wore, even in burial. In this case, it seems most likely that Yeshua wrapped the child in his own talit before He commanded her to rise.

Either way, some questions come immediately to mind. If Mark had been writing in Greek, why would he include such a uniquely Hebrew phrase? Why not simply render the words of Yeshua directly in Greek, as he supposedly did with everything else in the book? It seems a lot more likely that this one phrase simply would not translate directly when it was re-rendered in Greek by someone without sufficient understanding of Hebrew to explain, in Greek, what really happened. Indeed, if the original language had been Greek this particular translation problem never would have arisen.

Another noted Hebrew authority, Dr. Daniel ben Gigi, has spent a lifetime studying the so-called "Greek writings" of the New Testament (*B'rit Hadashah*). To him there isn't any question that a significant portion of the B'rit Hadashah was written first in Hebrew. The Greek of the supposedly earliest texts is not even "standard" Greek, and certainly is not the classic Greek of the educated classes, which included men like Matthew, Luke, and John. The Greek of the New Testament is known as "translator's" Greek and was used only for the most rudimentary renderings of non-Greek texts.[8]

Finally, to give you just two or three more examples of the external evidence[9] with respect to Matthew's gospel, here's more of what David Bivin and Roy Blizzard, Jr., have to say:

The early church fathers are usually referred to as the Ante-Nicean Fathers, i.e., the leaders of the primitive Christian Church up to the Council of Nicea in approximately AD 325. Their testimony is important because it carries us back to the early centuries of the Christian era.

...Our earliest witness is Papias, Bishop of Hierapolis, in Asia Minor (mid-second century AD). Concerning the Hebrew origin of the Gospels, he states:

> Matthew put down the words of the Lord in the Hebrew language, and others have translated them, each as best he could (Eusebius, *Ecclesiastical History* III 39, 16).

Irenaeus (AD 120-202) was Bishop of Lyons in France. Most of his literary endeavors were undertaken in the last quarter of the second century AD

Irenaeus states:

> Matthew, indeed, produced his gospel written among the Hebrew in their own dialect (Eusebius, *Ecclesiastical History* VI 8, 2).

Origen (first quarter of the third century), in his commentary on Matthew, states:

> The first [gospel], composed in the Hebrew language, was written by Matthew...for those who came to faith from Judaism (Eusebius, *Ecclesiastical History* VI 25, 4).

Eusebius, Bishop of Caesarea (circa AD 325), writes:

> Matthew had first preached to the Hebrews, and when he was about to go to others also, he transmitted his gospel in writing in his native language (*Ecclesiastical History* III 24,6).

These are but a few of the references in the writings of the early church fathers that indicate a Hebrew original for the gospels. In addition to these, there are many references in the later church fathers (the post-Nicean Fathers, from approximately AD 325). Epiphanius [died AD 420], for instance, writes at length about the Jewish-Christian sect of the Nazarenes:

> They have the entire Gospel of Matthew in Hebrew. It is carefully preserved by them as it was originally written, in Hebrew script (*Refutation of All Heresies* 29, 9, 4).[10]

Finally, the eminent third-century scholar, Jerome, said:

> Matthew was the first in Judea to compose the gospel of Christ in Hebrew letters and words . . . Who it was that later translated it into Greek is no longer known with certainty. Furthermore, the Hebrew text itself is still preserved in the library at Caesarea which the martyr Pamphilus assembled with great care (*De Viris Inlustribus 3*).[11]

Who wants to argue with Jerome?

Phonic *and* pictographic

Let us explain some additional things about the actual language that most of the Bible was written in. Most written languages are either *phonic* or *pictographic*. In the modern era, many Eastern languages are pictographic while most Western languages are phonic.[12]

However, both concepts came together in ancient biblical Hebrew, which is the *only language in the world* that represents words and meanings *simultaneously*, in both of those two fundamentally different yet complementary ways.[13]

- **First**, ancient Hebrew uses an alphabetic system to form words. They are pronounced as successive, right-to-left letter aggregations, or "sound blendings," of the sounds assigned to those letters. That's a fancy way of saying that, if you know the sounds of the Hebrew letters, you can reproduce the correct sounds of a Hebrew word even if you don't actually know its meaning. But you'd be doing exactly the same thing that a first-grader in America might do after he learns that, in English, the letter C, followed by the letter A, followed by the letter T, would be read as "CAT." That wouldn't necessarily mean that he would know what a cat is; only that he could decipher simple arrangements of the code we use to represent English-language words on the page.
- **Second**, Hebrew is also a "pictographic" language.[14] Every letter in the ancient Hebrew alephbet has manifold meanings of its own. Many of those meanings are also embodied within the shape of the letter itself. So, the ancient letter *gimel* means *camel* and looks like one. The ancient letter *dalet* means *door* and looks like one. And the ancient letter *ayin* means *eye* and – you guessed it – also looks like one.

The second letter in Hebrew is *bet*. As shown in Table 1-1,[15] when "sounded out" bet is identical to the English letter B. But its pictographic meaning(s) include at least three separate concepts: *house, in,* or *family*.

Table 1-1: Hebrew Letters[1]

Hebrew Letter	Hebrew Name	Phonic Sound, in English	Pictographic Meaning	English Counterpart
א	aleph	ah	first; strong; leader	A
ב	bet	/b/	house	B
כ	chaf	/k/	open hand	K
מ	mem	/m/	chaos	M
שׁ	shin	/sh/	consume; devour	Sh
ר	resh	/r/	man; person; head	R
ת	tav	/t/	sign of the covenant	T

The result of bringing alphabetic characters and pictographs together is that virtually every combination of Hebrew letters contains within itself its own meaning. So, when you draw a bet (/b/) in Hebrew you're committing not only to a *sound* but to a *concept* as well. To put it another way, every word that has a bet (/b/) sound in it also has the "bet" concept embedded within itself. Thus the smallest Hebrew word can contain literally volumes of meaning.

So, in Revelation 1:8, when Yeshua said what English translations usually render with the alphabetic letters given in Greek, as "I am the Alpha and Omega" (which we take to mean "beginning and end"), what He actually said in the original Hebrew was, "I am the aleph and the tav."

In addition to that, the ancient tav was shaped like a cross, representing a biblical prophecy to the effect that Messiah would die on a tree (i.e., a "cross"), which wasn't even a known form of execution when this prophecy was written.

Thus He was making a much larger statement than the words themselves seem to imply in either Greek or English. Because, in addition to *beginning*, the Hebrew letter *aleph* also means that He was the *first*, He was *strong*, and He was the *leader*. And the Hebrew word/letter *tav*, in addition to *end*, also means *sign of the covenant*. And, of course, he was looking ahead to the exact means by which He would die.

In other words, Yeshua actually did say that He was the beginning and the end. But He also said that He was the first (meaning that He was present when the universe was created), He was strong, He was the leader, and He was literally both the "sign" of the ultimate covenant with man (see chapter two) and its fulfillment as well.

Here are some additional examples of the English equivalents of Hebrew words, with their corresponding meanings also shown in English, as revealed entirely "within themselves" by the Hebrew letters that form the words in the Hebrew language.

Table 1-2: Hebrew Words

Hebrew Word	English Equivalent	Meaning Contained Within the Hebrew Letters/Pictographs
Shalom	Peace	Destroy the authority that binds us to chaos
Dot	Religion	Doorway to the sign of the covenant
Satan	Adversary	A snake that devours life
Elohim	God	The first, or strong, authority revealed
Shomer	Watchman	One who consumes the chaos of man
Torah	Bible*	To reveal the man nailed to the cross

*We use this word here to help connect the concept of "Torah" to the concept of "Bible."

The original language

The original text of the book of Genesis strongly implies that God actually used ancient Hebrew when He spoke the world into existence. In the very first verse it says:

בְּרֵאשִׁית   בָּרָא   אֱלֹהִים   אֵת
In the beginning   he created   God   **

הַשָּׁמַיִם   וְאֵת   הָאָרֶץ
the heavens   and   the earth.

The fourth word He spoke, indicated by the two asterisks above (**), was spelled aleph-tav and was pronounced "et." This word is normally not even translated into English at all, since there's no corresponding concept in our own language. Nevertheless, it definitely does have a pictographic meaning, and other implications as well.

By the inclusion of that word (sometimes described as a "binding" word by teachers of Hebrew) in the very middle of the first sentence of the first book of the Bible, God was further identifying who He was – "I am the first and the last, the first sign of covenant." In addition, that same word also means "the beginning and the end and everything in between." Thus, on another level, God could have been saying that He created the aleph and the tav, and all the letters in between – in other words, that He created the Hebrew language even before He created the physical world.

Yeshua reinforced all this in the last book of the Bible when He claimed to be the same *et*, meaning that He was the same creator God who created everything in the beginning. Thus, in the first chapter of Revelation He clearly linked Himself with the same God and the same act of creation, but in a way that only someone who understands Hebrew could fully comprehend and appreciate.

More examples

Let us give you three more quick examples of how much we miss when we don't fully understand the Hebrew underpinnings of the Bible.

1) Three separate words in Hebrew translate as "create," each with very specific refinements in meaning. The author of Genesis understood this and used each word accordingly, as follows:

   ◆ The first of the three words, "bara"[16] (which was literally the second word used in the Bible), means to create something from nothing. This word is reserved for God alone, for He is the only one who has ever successfully challenged the first law of thermodynamics. In its simplest form, this "law" claims that "Nothing can be created from nothing." Obviously, someone forgot to explain that to God.

   ◆ The second word, "yetzer,"[17] means to create something from raw materials that already exist. This word was first used in Genesis for the creation of Adam.

   ◆ The third word, "ben" (Genesis 2:22), is a form of creating and means children, or offspring. So Eve is a child of Adam, was "made" from Adam, in his image, with the same genetic structure, etc.[18] This word was first used when God reached into Adam's "inner court," his "side chamber," to extract a rib and create a woman. In other words, woman is a refined version of man.

2) Some commentators have promoted Greek as the language of the New Testament so aggressively that they've even claimed that Yeshua spoke the word "teleo," Greek for "It is finished," on the cross at 3 o'clock in the afternoon. This is hopelessly incorrect. What He actually said, in Hebrew, would be transliterated as "Nagmar," a one-purpose-and-one-purpose-only word reserved for the exclusive use of the high priest, who said it twice on the day of the Passover.

   The high priest said it the first time when he sacrificed the *first* Passover lamb at 9 o'clock that morning, precisely when Yeshua was nailed to the cross. He said it the second time, with his arms spread wide as Yeshua's were on the cross, when he sacrificed the *last* of the Passover lambs at precisely 3 o'clock in the afternoon, the same hour that Yeshua died.

God was into symbolism in a big way! Given all that richness built into the context, it's hard to understand how any commentator could ignore it and work so hard to give Yeshua's last earthly hours and words a Greek spin. Clearly, we miss much if we do not look at these verses from a Hebraic orientation.

3) In the King James translation of Matthew 11:11–12 we find the following:

> Verily I say unto you, Among them that are born of women there hath not risen a greater than John the Baptist: notwithstanding he that is least in the kingdom of heaven is greater than he. And from the days of John the Baptist until now the kingdom of heaven suffereth violence, and the violent take it by force.

Various commentators have misinterpreted the last sentence, above, for hundreds of years. The Amplified Bible even adds the words "as a precious prize – a share in the heavenly kingdom is sought with most ardent zeal and intense exertion" to the end of it. But in reality, these verses refer directly to a passage found in Micah 2:12–13:

> I will surely assemble, O Jacob, all of thee; I will surely gather the remnant of Israel; I will put them together as the sheep of Bozrah, as the flock in the midst of their fold: they shall make great noise by reason of the multitude of men. The breaker is come up before them: they have broken up, and have passed through the gate, and are gone out by it: and their king shall pass before them, and the LORD on the head of them. (KJV)

In the original Hebrew, the word translated as "breaker" is *peretz*, meaning either a shepherd who breaks boundaries to release his sheep ("breaching forth") or a woman going into labor (a birthing term).

Typically, an ancient Hebrew shepherd penned his sheep up each night, within an enclosure made of rocks. When it came time to let them loose in the morning, the shepherd (i.e., the "breaker") would knock out some of the stones in the wall with his staff. The sheep themselves would then expand the breach in the process of escaping, as they were set free or "birthed."

In a similar way, this passage explains that, in response to Yeshua, the Kingdom of Heaven is "bursting forth." It is clearly a Messianic reference; Yeshua is saying, "I smashed the rock out and birthed you forth; I am the shepherd who breaks down the walls and sets you free."

When the Greek words that are commonly translated as "the kingdom of heaven suffereth violence, and the violent take it by force" are translated back into what was undoubtedly the original Hebrew, they become an idiomatic expression (as described above) that lines up perfectly with what Micah was saying.

In other words, the whole thing makes no sense at all in the standard Hebrew-to-Greek-to-English sequence. Only when the Greek is translated directly back into Hebrew, and then directly into English, does it ring true.

Origins and accuracy

We want to conclude this chapter with a few words about the veracity of Scripture itself. To us it's a given that all Holy Scripture was directly inspired by God, and written down exactly as He wanted the words to be. In that belief we agree completely with the writer of Hebrews, who said in Hebrews 4:12:

> For the word of God is living and active and sharper
> than any two-edged sword, and piercing as far as
> the division of soul and spirit, of both joints and
> marrow, and able to judge the thoughts and inten-
> tions of the heart.[19]

On the other hand, given how many centuries have passed
during which the Scriptures have been copied and recopied countless times on animal skins, paper, and any number of other
materials, we need to understand a few additional things.

First, no one still has the original documents. However, we do
have many *very early handwritten copies of the Old Testament*, made
by ancient Hebrew scribes who worked within an incredibly strict
system. Each scribe was overseen by up to 120 of the greatest
scholars of the day. All were members of the Knesset Hagadol, or
"Great Assembly," and each scribe underwent rigorous training
roughly equivalent to that of a rabbi.

These scholars viewed each scroll as it was written. Everything
was double- and triple-checked, and any scroll that contained more
than one error was taken out and buried where it quickly rotted
away. Thus scrupulous accuracy was guaranteed despite the human
dimension. From scrolls produced between AD 500 and AD 1500,
modern scholars can extrapolate backwards and certify that the Old
Testament is close to one hundred percent accurate.

> "There is thus no reasonable doubt that our present
> Old Testament, based on the Masoretic text, is prac-
> tically identical with the text in use several centuries
> before Christ, practically extending back to the time
> when the last books of the Old Testament were origi-
> nally written. That being true, there is no reason to
> doubt that all the books have come down to us as
> substantially written."[20]
> "One can find scores of published testimonials by
> reputable scholars who, as a result of their studies
> of the Dead Sea Scrolls have declared their surprise
> that the changes the Masoretic Text experienced in

the course of transmission were so few and so insignificant. Professor Albright said in this respect that the Dead Sea Scrolls proved 'conclusively that we must treat the consonantal text of the Hebrew Bible with the utmost respect and that the free amending of difficult passages in which modern critical scholars have indulged cannot be tolerated any longer.'"[21]

On the other hand, starting with the very first transcriptions, the New Testament was copied under a completely different system. Because it was not part of Torah, the New Testament got completely outside the ancient Hebrew transcription system. The Greeks had nothing to compare to that system, to guarantee the New Testament's integrity. When the Roman Catholic Church took over the process around AD 300, they also had no similar methods, so things did not get any better.

What does that mean to us today? Well, our beloved King James Version is the perfect example. It was based on Greek copies of the whole Bible (and not the oldest Hebrew copies produced by the Hebrew scribes), all of which were produced between AD 1200 and AD 1500, by which point a number of errors had already crept in.

Given the above, all of which is known to biblical scholars, it's hard to understand why many modern students of the Bible still use a Greek text, knowing that most of the original was written in Hebrew. And, knowing further that highly accurate, completely legitimate copies of the original Old Testament are freely available.

What do we use?

That's easy! For the Old Testament we use an accurately reproduced copy of the original Hebrew.[22] In fact, many of the examples in this book come directly from that. By contrast, when we're working in B'rit Hadashah (the Hebrew name for the New Testament, which we'll discuss more fully in the next chapter) we sometimes use a reverse translation of the Greek text, one prepared by translators who examined the oldest Greek text word-by-word [23] and substituted the normal Hebrew source words according to the translation standards of that day. The Hebrew idioms that sometimes emerge provide startling clarity for passages that have seemed obscure and "untranslatable" for centuries. At other times, for a quick "sense" of the Scriptures we use the Amplified Version. It's not the most graceful translation, but clarity is much more important than elegance.[24]

One final thing we want to make very clear before we leave this chapter. You must understand that the Jewish-Hebrew source of our Bible is a *huge* subject and cannot be dealt with adequately in the confines of this book. If you're the least bit doubtful about anything we say in these pages, we urge you to go to the bibliography at the end of the book, select any of the dozens of books we've listed there on the subject in question, and *get independent verification of what we've said.*

Most of these books are utterly fascinating. But more important, you really need to read at least *some* of them for yourself so you can see how extensive and well-documented the evidence really is.

What's in a name?

One more important point that flows from all we have said so far. In Matthew 1:21, an angel of the Lord told the virgin Mary (actually, in both Hebrew and English her name would be *Miriam* – or *Miryam*, as it's sometimes transliterated) to name her unborn child *Yeshua*, which means "I am Salvation." Mary/Miriam then used that name when she called her son in for lunch.

In the 2,000 years since Yeshua's birth, any number of complicated explanations have come along to explain how "Yeshua" became "Jesus Christ." Here's what we consider the most likely sequence:

(Hebrew)		(Greek)		(Latin)		(English)
Yeshua	=	Iesous	=	Jesu	=	Jesus

However, in keeping with our emphasis on textual and linguistic accuracy, tempered by deep respect for *Who He really was* (and still is!), we have taken the liberty of bypassing all that.

Therefore, most of the time, in this and subsequent volumes, we will continue to refer to "Jesus" by His given name, *Yeshua*. And by His given title, as well . . . *Messiah.*

In summary . . .

- ◆ Most of us approach the Scriptures innocently and unknowingly, from the classic Babylonian-Roman-Greek perspective. And yet, with a few extremely minor exceptions, all of the Old Testament and much of the New was written in ancient Hebrew, by Hebrew men. There isn't a "Western" author in the crowd!
- ◆ The ancient Hebrew language is both phonic-driven and pictographic. The letters themselves have intrinsic meaning. Each word is literally defined by the letters that comprise it, and therefore contains within itself its own meaning.
- ◆ The ancient Hebrew scribes worked within a complex, highly organized transcription system that guaranteed accurate copies of the original Scriptures. Nothing like it existed anywhere else, including the world of the Romans, the Greeks, and the monasteries of the Catholic Church. Unfortunately, these latter groups were the ones who produced most of the copies of Scripture that scholars use today to produce our English language paraphrases.
- ◆ Proper understanding of the Scriptures requires two things. First, you need to be willing to go back to the original Hebrew text and research key words and phrases. Second, you also need to study the ancient Hebrew culture. Content without context is simply not enough.

2

Covenant

I want to start this chapter with something very unusual in a book of this type. To make what I consider a very important point, I want to quote a short section from chapter two of *The Adventures of Huckleberry Finn*, the Mark Twain classic from 1885. Tom Sawyer is the speaker in the first sentence; the other characters are all young boys of Tom's age, including Huck himself who is also the narrator.

> "Now, we'll start this band of robbers and call it Tom Sawyer's Gang. Everybody that wants to join has got to take an oath, and write his name in blood."
>
> Everybody was willing. So Tom got out a sheet of paper that he had wrote the oath on, and read it. It swore every boy to stick to the band, and never tell any of the secrets; and if anybody done anything to any boy in the band, whichever boy was ordered to kill that person and his family must do it, and he mustn't eat and he mustn't sleep till he had killed them and hacked a cross in their breasts, which was the sign of the band. And nobody that didn't belong to the band could use that mark, and if he did he must be sued; and if he done it again he must be killed. And if anybody that belonged to the band

told the secrets, he must have his throat cut, and then have his carcass burnt up and the ashes scattered all around, and his name blotted off of the list with blood and never mentioned again by the gang, but have a curse put on it and be forgot forever.

Everybody said it was a real beautiful oath, and asked Tom if he got it out of his own head. He said, some of it, but the rest was out of pirate-books and robber-books, and every gang that was high-toned had it.

Some thought it would be good to kill the families of boys that told the secrets. Tom said it was a good idea, so he took a pencil and wrote it in. Then Ben Rogers says:

"Here's Huck Finn, he hain't got no family; what you going to do 'bout him?"

"Well, hain't he got a father?" says Tom Sawyer.

"Yes, he's got a father, but you can't never find him these days. He used to lay drunk with the hogs in the tanyard, but he hain't been seen in these parts for a year or more."

They talked it over, and they was going to rule me out, because they said every boy must have a family or somebody to kill, or else it wouldn't be fair and square for the others. Well, nobody could think of anything to do — everybody was stumped, and set still. I was most ready to cry; but all at once I thought of a way, and so I offered them Miss Watson — they could kill her. Everybody said:

"Oh, she'll do. That's all right. Huck can come in."

Then they all stuck a pin in their fingers to get blood to sign with, and I made my mark on the paper.

Why do I quote the above? Because, even as Mark Twain put the finishing touches on his own manuscript in 1885, Dr. Clay Trumbull delivered a series of three lectures to the Episcopal Divinity School in Philadelphia, Pennsylvania, in the same year. The subject of those lectures was the same subject explored by the fictional Tom and Huck, above.

Dr. Trumbull traced the origin and development of the oldest form of covenant known to man. Those teachings were then converted into a different kind of book altogether, called *Blood Covenant*. Like Twain's classic, Trumbull's book has also never been equaled in more than 115 years, but there the resemblance ends.

A covenant is not a testament

As the Trumbull book demonstrated for all time, covenant is a *huge* subject. It's also an ancient subject, an ubiquitous subject (meaning that it shows up somewhere in almost every civilization that ever existed), and a very serious subject that has been on the minds of men far longer than anyone can remember. It's also a subject that few modern Bible students seem to understand.

For example, many of us confuse *covenant* and *testament*. In fact, as was true of both the Greek and the Roman cultures, some dictionaries even today seem barely able to differentiate between the two. And yet, in ancient Hebrew society (the context in which the Bible was written), those two words never meant the same thing.

A testament is a Greek legal document that defines the lawful rights of all those to whom it applies. A Last Will and Testament, in which someone details his wishes for the disposition of his property after his death, is a prime example. In such a case, the Greek practice of giving greatest weight to the most recent such "testament" makes good sense. Legally, any *new* testament makes null and void any *previous* (i.e., "old") testament by the same party. A newer Will always supercedes an older Will.

By contrast, the word *covenant* defines *an ongoing relationship with no appointed end.* Rather than being a legal document, a covenant is a commitment to develop a certain kind of *continuing relationship.* By its very existence it implies a dynamic interaction between partners, a growing organic process.

Given that, there's really no legitimate way to use the words "new covenant" to imply that you are somehow trotting out a new one to replace an old one, as you might send in a backup to replace a quarterback with a broken leg. You can adapt an existing covenant by adding additional conditions, but you can't terminate it (i.e., declare it null and void) and replace it with a different (or "new") one.

(This, of course, is exactly what so many misguided believers attempt to do when they claim that the New Testament replaced the Old, but that's another story entirely.)

So forget the "new" concept. The Hebrew name for the Gospels and the books that follow (i.e., from Matthew through Revelation) is *B'rit Hadashah* (Jeremiah 31:31–34). The Hebrew word *B'rit* means "covenant,"[1] which is further defined as "to eat together, to share food, to prepare a banquet."[2] What comes to mind is a picture of friends and family, interacting and sharing a meal together. The ancient Hebrews recognized their responsibility to provide a meal whenever a guest entered their homes. They were also responsible to protect the life and possessions of anyone who came inside their home, as demonstrated so poignantly in the story of Lot and the two angelic strangers he entertained.

> Now the two angels came to Sodom in the evening as Lot was sitting in the gate of Sodom. When Lot saw them, he rose to meet them and bowed down with his face to the ground. And he said, "Now behold, my lords, please turn aside into your servant's house, and spend the night, and wash your feet; then you may rise early and go on your way." They said however, "No, but we shall spend the night in the square." Yet he urged them strongly, so they turned aside to him and entered his house; and he prepared a feast for them, and baked unleavened bread, and they ate. (Genesis 19:1–3)

B'rit also means "to cleanse or make pure," and "a son of the sign."[3] When God called Abraham into a deeper relationship, He asked him to circumcise himself as a sign of the covenant relationship between them (Genesis 17:11). Circumcision was also an outward sign of the purity (i.e., the holiness) that God imputed to Abraham at that time. Thus, Abraham and his descendants became "sons of the sign."

In Hebrew, *hadashah* means "renewed" or "a cycle of restoration," or "to return to a previous state."[4] The same word is also used in reference to the lunar cycle, meaning that we don't get a new moon every month – the old one just gets restored to a previous condition. The same thing is true of B'rit Hadashah, meaning that *somewhere in the history of covenant we've been here before!*

Therefore, a more accurate title for the New Testament would be "Renewed Covenant," or "Renewed Relationship," not "New Covenant" as the original Hebrew in Jeremiah 31:31–34 is commonly mistranslated:

> "Behold, days are coming," declares the LORD, "when I will make a new covenant with the house of Israel and with the house of Judah, not like the covenant which I made with their fathers in the day I took them by the hand to bring them out of the land of Egypt, My covenant which they broke, although I was a husband to them," declares the LORD. "But this is the covenant which I will make with the house of Israel after those days," declares the LORD, "I will put My law within them and on their heart I will write it; and I will be their God, and they shall be My people. "They will not teach again, each man his neighbor and each man his brother, saying, 'Know the LORD,' for they will all know Me, from the least of them to the greatest of them," declares the LORD, "for I will forgive their iniquity, and their sin I will remember no more."

Again, this means something entirely different from what we imply when we call the last 24 books of the Bible by their Greek-based title, "The New Testament." For unlike a testament, in which the legal aspects of *contract* are everything, a *covenant's* contractual elements play only a small part.

Our arbitrary attempts at organizing Scripture into two halves also have no real significance whatsoever. From God's perspective there is no such thing as what we call the Old Testament and the New Testament. He created Scripture to define His all-inclusive, all-encompassing plan of redemption as an ongoing covenant between Himself and us. The defining document for that single, unified, divine plan is the Holy Bible. Period.

God's plan unveiled

In the Scriptures, the unveiling of God's plan begins with the first chapter of Genesis and ends with the last chapter of Revelation. Nothing supercedes or eliminates anything else as the plan unfolds. "Contractual legalities" are few and far between. Therefore, the Bible is not in any significant sense whatsoever a Greek testament. It's not Greek; again the terms "Old Testament" and "New Testament" simply do not apply.

Those terms were imposed on the Bible in the second century by the early church fathers. At that point, most of them were converted Greek philosophers with no Hebraic roots. Apparently they also had precious little understanding of where "their" Bible came from.

The Old and New Testament labels were unfortunate distractions from God's plan. They have created ongoing misunderstandings that have now persevered for almost two thousand years. They imply that the Old Testament became less important, or was even "cancelled" the moment the New Testament joined the "canon."

To illustrate my point, in AD 153, Ignatius of Rome wrote in *A Letter to the Philadelphians* that "The Old Testament is good, the New Testament is better. The Old Testament is the imperfect, waiting for the perfect to replace it."

If the Apostle Paul had heard that about his letters to the Greeks he would have rolled over in his grave! To cite just one familiar example, in 2 Timothy 3:16, Paul said: "All Scripture is inspired by God and profitable for teaching, for reproof, for correction, for training in righteousness."

When did these writings "come from the mouth of God"? When He spoke forth Torah on Mount Sinai, which is about as "Old Testament" as you can get! In fact, when Paul wrote the above, much of the the so-called "New Testament" had not even been written yet. And none of it had been officially canonized.

The same is true of this passage from James 2:8: "If, however, you are fulfilling the royal law according to the Scripture, "YOU SHALL LOVE YOUR NEIGHBOR AS YOURSELF," you are doing well." The "Scripture" James referred to was, undeniably, the Old Testament.

Some of this reminds us of what Harry Truman said a half-century ago, when someone responded to one of his diatribes with "Give 'em hell, Harry!"

"I don't give 'em hell," he said. "I just tell the truth on 'em, and they *think* it's hell!"

Oh, that someone would have told the truth and "Given them hell" on these false ideas many years ago! And many more, too, that will come up in the pages ahead.

Reinforcing important truths

Now, nothing we've said above is meant to imply that any of what happened was the fault of Ignatius alone. By the time he wrote the lines we quoted several paragraphs above, the Greeks had already set in motion this fundamental shift in how the next ninety-some generations of believers would view their own Holy Scriptures.

To review some of what we've said so far, a more accurate English title for the New Testament would be "Renewed Relationship" or "Renewed Covenant," reflecting two essential realities about ancient Biblical covenant.

1) **First**, since the nature of covenant is never to become null and void, each "renewed" covenant includes everything that came before. God's promises are eternal. So a new or renewed covenant (e.g., the so-called "New Testament") does not invalidate those that preceded it (e.g., the so-called "Old Testament"); it simply includes and expands them.

2) **Second**, when a covenant is renewed it may then contain additional and/or expanded provisions, but they are folded into the existing covenant, which (of course!) still remains in force.

Defining covenant types

In Exodus 23:31 through 24:8, God referred to the first five books of the Old Testament (also called *Torah*, though the word Torah is also understood to mean the entire Old Testament) as the "Book of the Covenant" (Exodus 24:7). He also expressed great concern about our entering relationships that might lead us away from Him. In Torah, God enumerates seven progressive and inclusive covenants as a pattern of restoration for mankind. These seven covenants are represented by the following four fundamental covenant *types*.

Blood Covenant

The first fundamental type is called *blood* covenant, which we've already mentioned several times. This relationship, also understood as "entering into a relationship of servanthood," requires the shedding of blood by sacrifice and must be renewed daily. As Paul said in I Corinthians 15:31: "I affirm, brethren, by the boasting in you which I have in Christ Jesus our Lord, I die daily."

To apprehend the same dynamic in more graphic terms, understand that man is at war with two propensities within himself. Many rabbis refer to them as the *yetzer tav* and the *yetzer hara*[5] – i.e., "good inclination, bad inclination" – and they often use the white dog/black dog analagy to describe that war. The dog you feed the most is the one that wins. This service covenant is a commitment we make to God to fight the good fight against our bad inclinations which, unchecked, would lead us into sin. Our positive, obedient actions "feed" the white dog, help us maintain our covenant with God, and are seen by Him as signs of honor.

Adam and Eve, in effect, were in a marriage covenant (detailed in chapter three) with God. When they disobeyed they effectively handed God a writ of divorce. In response, God sought to restore His highest-level covenant with them, in step-by-step fashion as we'll see later, first by shedding the blood of an animal to make clothes for them. Animal sacrifice, as defined by ancient biblical Hebrew culture, was also a symbol of restoration and purification. Thus the initial covenant relationship that God established with Adam and Eve, and Noah, was a blood (service) covenant (Genesis 9:7–17 and Genesis 3:17–22), the first step on their pathway toward restoration.

Incidentally, we often assume that the animal was a sheep, for the word used in Hebrew actually meant "wooly animal." But we don't really know for sure. Either way, God was conveying to Adam and Eve that the beginning of their restoration involved going back to the beginning . . . servanthood and obedience.

Likewise, Noah made a blood sacrifice after the Flood waters receded. In so doing he fulfilled man's half of the original blood covenant between God and mankind. God originated it; now man reciprocated. Noah is an obvious example of the faithful servant who did what God required.

In other words, by asking us to enter into a servant relationship with Himself, God is asking us to serve and obey Him. As Luke said,

So you too, when you do all the things which are
commanded you, say, 'We are unworthy slaves; we
have done only that which we ought to have done.'
(Luke 17:10)

Additional scriptures, supporting the above, would include
Revelation 22:12; 2 Corinthians 5:10; Matthew 16:27, 25:14-30;
James 2:14-18.

It's worth noting that wine is considered an acceptable Hebrew
alternative to shedding blood; it's the "blood of the grape." That
explains why we currently observe communion as we do. Through
the wine we are constantly renewing the blood covenant that God
initiated with Adam so many years ago, and renewed with the death
of Yeshua.

Salt Covenant

The second type of covenant is called *salt* covenant.[6] In contrast
to the blood covenant (wherein Paul died daily), this is an *eternal* covenant. Once you make it, it's "made" forever and doesn't
have to be renewed constantly. Its name comes from an ancient
practice. Each Hebrew person carried a small pouch of salt. When
two or more men wanted to enter into this type of relationship
with each other, the parties to the covenant would mix their salt
in a common bowl, break bread, dip it into the salt, and eat it.
When they were finished they would redistribute the salt into
their pouches.

At that point, the only way to break the covenant would be to
separate each grain of salt from the others and return it to its original owner. Since this was impossible, the established bond had to
remain . . . forever.

Salt covenant, also called both the covenant of *hospitality* and
the covenant of *friendship,* was represented by the breaking of
salted bread, and by fellowship. God wants to restore the lost
friendship and closeness this type of relationship offers. When

we enter into a salt covenant with God, He expands on the servanthood covenant (i.e., the blood covenant) and rewards us with more of Himself.

When Abraham welcomed the Lord and broke bread with Him (Genesis 18:1–15), he was modeling the salt covenant. As with the blood covenant, the salt covenant begins at God's initiation. God pursued Abraham and gave him a unilateral promise. But at the same time, God still required Abraham to do certain things. And Abraham was still modeling servant (i.e., blood) covenant when he raised the knife and almost sacrificed Isaac.

This again demonstrates the progressive, cumulative nature of covenant. Abraham's original blood covenant with God (Genesis 15:5–21) wasn't cancelled or replaced by his salt covenant with God. For once you enter salt covenant you become a friend of the one you're in covenant with, but you also continue to be a servant. Abraham was called a "friend of God" but he never stopped being a servant.

It's also worth noting that, when God promised to make Abraham into a great nation, He was also promising him a huge inheritance, which leads into the next covenant. We bring that point up here to show that God often makes a promise to be fulfilled in later generations, even as the sower reaps in a later season.

Just as the persistence of someone like Jacob (who asked God to "fix" or "bless" him in his heart [Genesis 32:26], and wrestled with the Lord until he got what he wanted) is a picture of the friendship covenant, the persistence and patience of God is shown in the "long view of history" that God always takes.

Sandal covenant

The third type of covenant is *sandal* covenant, also called the covenant of *inheritance*. The ancient Hebrews used worn-out sandals to mark the boundaries of their property. They partially covered them with rocks to hold them in place against the natural elements.

However, any such "weighing down" was not intended to hold the sandals in place against human interference. Moving boundaries was strictly forbidden by divine command, as set forth in Deuteronomy 19:14: "You shall not move your neighbor's boundary mark, which the ancestors have set, in your inheritance which you will inherit in the land that the LORD your God gives you to possess."[7]

Over time, sandals themselves came to represent the inheritance concept. Thus the sandal covenant is a picture of the relationship of sons and daughters with their parents.

Along with the privilege of inheritance comes the responsibility to maintain the servant covenant as well. In ancient Hebrew households, during the day you could not tell the sons and daughters apart from the hired help. But at dinnertime the difference became obvious; the sons and daughters were the ones sitting with the parents at the family table.

Inheritance also requires us to be a good steward of our Father's estate. This was God's original intent for Adam and Eve in the Garden of Eden. They were given the authority and the reponsibility to manage the garden and the earth, but lost out through disobedience.

Nonetheless, God still plans to restore our authority through the renewal of this type of covenant, as promised in Revelation 20 when the bride sits with Yeshua on the throne and rules and reigns with Him.

Another example

In the book of Ruth, chapter 4:1–13, we see how the closest relative of Ruth chose not to purchase her family's field, nor to take her as his wife. Instead, he allowed Ruth's cousin Boaz to acquire both the land and Ruth, and yielded his right to possession by removing his sandal and handing it to Boaz. Moses understood the same symbolism when he was commanded by God to remove his sandals – his man-made earthly inheritance – and to receive from the Lord a *new* inheritance of holiness (Exodus 3:5), which the children of Israel entered into when they took possession of the

Promised Land. David typifies the Inheritance Covenant because, as king, he and his descendants inherited the throne eternally, as promised in Psalm 132:11,12:

> [11] The LORD has sworn to David
> A truth from which He will not turn back:
> "Of the fruit of your body I will set upon your throne.
> [12] "If your sons will keep My covenant
> And My testimony which I will teach them,
> Their sons also shall sit upon your throne forever."

To take an example from B'rit Hadashah, the story of the rich young ruler (Matthew 19:16–29) shows us what Yeshua is looking for in someone who aspires to be both a servant and a friend. The young man was obedient to God's commandments, but he found it difficult to enter into Yeshua's offer of a deeper relationship.

Yeshua basically said, "You are already my servant and my friend; now come and be my son." But the young man wasn't quite ready to trade his earthly inheritance for an increased share in the heavenly kingdom. Therefore, his poor decision prevented him from entering into a deeper relationship and getting any farther than the friendship (salt) covenant.

This does not mean, by the way, that the rich young ruler "lost out" on what he had settled with God up to that moment. His salvation was never in question. But like so many believers today, who are called into deeper relationships, the rich young ruler simply failed to draw closer when the opportunity came.

Table 2-1 shows how three basic types of covenants were modeled in the Old Testament. Bear in mind that the *first step in each covenant always comes at God's initiative.* The second half comes when *man reciprocates,* which doesn't always happen immediately. But God always waits patiently for the opportunity to reward His people as soon as they respond to His promptings.

To amplify just one of these examples, Moses received the promise from God but he was also called to a much deeper level of responsibility. He was given the Torah, the highest precepts and

Table 2-1: Patriarchal Covenants

Type	God's Initiative	Sign	Man's Response	Sign	Comments
Blood, or Service	God created **Adam** and **Eve**, gave them the Garden of Eden, and asked them to serve Him. When they failed, God shed the blood of an animal to cover them.	Skins	**Noah** obeyed God and was righteous in God's sight. **Noah** also offered a blood sacrifice.	Rainbow	Adam and **Eve** were once innocent, but when they sinned they had no way to undo what they'd done. Obligated to serve.
Salt, or Friendship	God sent Yeshua and two angels to offer **Abraham** an unconditional promise of eternal friendship, sealed by breaking bread with him.	Circumcision	**Jacob** wrestled with God for the blessing	New Name, from Jacob to Israel	**Jacob** wanted the promises and the blessing – he pursued God. He had faced weaknesses within himself and wrestled for his inheritance. Obligated to defend.
Sandal, or Inheritance	God invited **Moses** to approach the burning bush and take off his sandals. God promised to deliver Israel and make Israel a nation of kings and priests.	Torah	**David** received the inheritance in spite of his sins, for which he still paid a big price	Kingship (Crown)	**Moses** was given the Torah, while **David** walked in it. Obligated to manage.
Betrothal, or Marriage	God gave us **Yeshua the Messiah** — Torah in the flesh.	Tav Covenant Signature (cross)	Acceptance by faith and keeping self pure	White Garments	Many are called but few are chosen (Matthew 22:14). Obligated to all three covenants, in perpetuity and maturity, as an equal partner.

*We have devoted an entire chapter (and much of the remainder of this book and the next one as well) to the betrothal or "marriage" covenant, which represents the culmination of all the above.

writings, and he was told to model them, to work them out, to get them in his soul. David was the direct fulfillment, for he was given the eternal throne.

At the same time, there was then no greater responsibility than being king of the nation of Israel. Ownership and stewardship of the land was a big deal. David and the Israelites were given the management of the land and expected to model what will happen when the whole world is brought into the picture.

Covenants are progressive

On a more human level, an earthly parent models the same series of covenants through his or her growing relationship with a son or daughter. If the parent does a good job of training a child in obediance (blood covenant), the child will become a friend (salt covenant). A son or daughter who matures and becomes a responsible adult eventually qualifies for an inheritance (sandal covenant).

As with the covenants we make with God, progressing to the salt and sandal covenants is a major goal of parenting, but neither one is where effective parenting begins. If you start by being a child's friend instead of training him or her in obediance, you have the whole thing backwards and it won't work.

Likewise in our evolving covenants with God. The relationship offered by each of the preceding covenants makes the *next* covenant possible. And all of this leads into a major point, repeated many times already: As *we enter into each new or "renewed" covenant with God we do not leave behind the responsibilities – or the benefits – of the preceding one.*

All these covenants point us to that oft-mentioned *progressive nature* of our purification, relationship, and partnership with God. However, we do not acquire our salvation through any "works" connected with each covenant. Only Yeshua's death on the cross, and our acceptance of His forgiveness, provide for that (John 3:14–18) for everyone ever born.

To illustrate this literally, recall the Last Supper in the Upper Room, as described in John 13:4–14. Yeshua offered the inheritance of His heavenly kingdom to His disciples. By removing their sandals and washing their feet He was giving them a new inheritance . . . His own. He was establishing a relationship of purity without manmade barriers, at the same time fulfilling the promise in John 1:12–13: "To them He gave power to become sons of God . . . " Some of the disciples protested at first, but His response was very clear: "If I don't do this you'll have no part of me."

Today, many believers think you can get saved and have all the intimacy you'll ever need by accepting the free gift, with no additional effort on your part. But salvation is only the beginning – it's only the first step toward establishing the intimacy that God desires. At that moment (or very soon thereafter), *God gives to each one of us the choice of increasing the maturity and intimacy of our relationship with Him.* This is the reality that many seem to miss.

Philippians 2:12 says, "work out your salvation [literally, 'work out your success'; terms of relationship, or obligations of covenant; i.e., purity] with fear and trembling [earnestness and urgency]." All of this takes on a whole new meaning when you begin to understand covenant.

The Lord will give us a step-by-step increase of His kingdom in our lives if we choose to walk out our faith. But we have to consciously make that commitment to move beyond basic salvation and enter into true covenant relationships with Him. When we do, He will give us the strength, the knowledge, and the stamina to move continually forward. As we show that we can be faithful with one step, He will show us the next.

The final step in the process of restoration is in the hand of the bridegroom alone. We will cover this in the next chapter, on betrothal/marriage. Why marriage? Because that is the ultimate fulfillment of all the covenants. God's goal for us is a marriage relationship with Himself, involving complete intimacy. Marriage is the renewed relationship He desires.

However, not everyone who accepts salvation will aspire to be His bride. Like the rich young prince, many will consider the price too high. But that will not leave them out in the cold – many people besides the bride and bridegroom will attend the wedding of the Lamb (Matthew 20:1–16, Matthew 22:1–14, Matthew 25:1–13, Revelation 19:5–9, Matthew 25:1–13). They just won't be part of the bride.

Because, you can't be married without being completely in covenant. Only when you've entered all three preceding types are you ready for marriage. And as you might expect, since the number seven represents biblical perfection, "perfect" covenant requires seven covenant phases, the six we've described above plus the ultimate marriage covenant itself.

How does color fit into all this?

One more concept we'd like to touch on before we close. As you'll hear us say over and over again, because He knows how our brains work, God is into symbolism in a big way. He is also into "layering," meaning that He has woven many threads of meaning into one gigantic tapestry of truth. God has found manifold ways to reinforce the things He wants us to know.

Color is also part of His Grand Scheme. We won't say much about it until we get to chapter nine, but here are some basic facts to keep in mind:

- God gave His "color" format to Noah, through the rainbow that He placed in the sky as Noah emerged from the ark.
- With respect to how colors that make up the spectrum relate to covenant, God's are the primary colors and man's are the secondary colors.
- Each of the covenants is represented by a primary color. Blood is red, raw salt is yellow, and inheritance is blue.

- The color of the ultimate covenant with God, betrothal, is white. White represents a combining of all the previous colors in the spectrum, just as the covenant itself represents a combining of all the previous covenants.

No man can serve two masters

A final "new" thought before we summarize. Whether you realize it or not, like everyone else on earth you are always in covenant with someone. The question is not *whether*, but *with whom?* It simply isn't possible to be neutral. By the very act of giving us free choice God required us to use it.

So . . . whose kingdom are you in? Whom do you obey? You can't be a servant of God and a servant of Satan at the same time, as Matthew 6:24 makes plain:

> No one can serve two masters; for either he will hate the one and love the other, or he will be devoted to one and despise the other. You cannot serve God and wealth.

At the same time, it might also be possible to consider yourself on one side but behave as though you belonged to the other. Consider Paul's words in his first letter to the Corinthians:

> Therefore whoever eats the bread or drinks the cup of the Lord in an unworthy manner, shall be guilty of the body and the blood of the Lord. But a man must examine himself, and in so doing he is to eat of the bread and drink of the cup. For he who eats and drinks, eats and drinks judgment to himself if he does not judge the body rightly. For this reason many among you are weak and sick, and a number sleep. (I Corinthians 11:27–30)

Obviously, the cup echoes service, the bread echoes friend-ship. But many of the Corinthians were not taking communion seriously – they were literally walking out the door and immedi-ately breaking the commitment to covenant that these symbols represented. This passage is conveying the seriousness of taking covenant too lightly. Falling asleep, in this context, is a metaphor for dying.

In summary . . .

- Covenant and testament are not the same thing. A cov-enant is a mutual agreement defining an ongoing relationship between the parties, without end. A testament is a legal contract defining the obligations between the par-ties, with a definite beginning and end.
- The Bible recognizes four main types of covenant – Ser-vice, Friendship, Inheritance, and Marriage, in that order. Each one involves a deeper, more intimate relationship than the one that went before. No "new" covenant replaces an old one; each one incorporates the provisions of the previ-ous one and builds accordingly.
- Yeshua modeled Communion, at Passover, via the wine, the bread, and foot washing, as our way of constantly re-newing the three covenants with God.
- Color plays an important part in the vast, unifying symbol-ogy that God created to help us understand His plan. It's a significant part of the covenants, but also of the additional concepts that lead to an understanding of the book of Rev-elation.

3

Betrothal

Every believer is familiar with the words of Revelation 3:20, from the King James Version of the Bible:

> Behold, I stand at the door, and knock: if any man hear my voice, and open the door, I will come in to him, and will sup with him, and he with me.

Most believers understand that verse to be the voice of Yeshua, reaching out to mankind. He's standing at their heart's door, asking to come in and save them from their sins.

That interpretation is true as far as it goes, but it certainly is not the whole story. Because most modern believers have almost no awareness of the ancient Hebrew culture in which the Old Testament and B'rit Hadashah were set, we often miss the true import of a thoroughly familiar, deeply meaningful, yet barely understood metaphor.

Let's talk about the background for that verse.

Ancient Hebrew betrothal

As we indicated in the previous chapter, marriage is the culmination of the three previous types of covenant: servanthood, friendship, and inheritance. That explains why the marriage relationship is so central to everything God ordained. In scripture after scripture, God identifies Himself as the Bridegroom, and He compares all those who enter into all three forms of covenant with Him as the bride. His own references to that fundamental image fill the Old Testament, from the stories of the patriarchs to the words He put in the mouths of His prophets.

Yeshua, John, Paul, and all the other Hebrew writers continued the same pattern all the way through B'rit Hadashah. References to the Hebrew marriage covenant, and to members of Christ's "church" as either *being* part of the bride or having the opportunity to *become* part of the bride ("many are called but few are chosen"), rise to a crescendo in Revelation.

The result is simple but dramatic. Just as you can't know Scripture if you don't know covenant, you can't truly understand covenant – and certainly not the book of Revelation – if you don't understand the ancient Hebrew marriage rituals and ceremony. So let's consider how it all works.

First of all, ancient Hebrew marriages were "arranged" but not in every tiny respect. Despite the *fait accompli* Tevye almost pulled off between his daughter and the butcher in *Fiddler on the Roof*, the ancient Hebrew bride and groom had more choice in the matter than many of us might realize. Parental approval was essential but the initial impetus often came from the young people themselves, who frequently knew exactly what (and whom!) they wanted.

Though a wedding in ancient Hebrew culture was a significant social and religious event, it was also part of a "process" involving commitment and covenant, the fulfillment of which often took several years. And many people were involved, including families on both sides, friends, and the rest of the community, each group having different responsibilities.

Often, a match was tentatively identified by the families as a mutually desirable outcome, sometimes years before the actual betrothal. However, any such "silent agreement" was not legally binding and was always subject to the would-be bride's approval.

But eventually, if all signals were "go" the prospective groom and his father would let it leak out to the bride's family that a formal proposal would soon be made.

On the day the prospective bridegroom made his first official move, he brought his father to the intended bride's house. They carried a betrothal cup, wine, and the anticipated bride price in a pouch. When they got there they knocked.

The prospective bride's father would be on the other side of the door, but before he opened it he would peek out through a little window, identify the visitors, then look to his daughter to confirm what, in most cases, she had long since settled in her own mind.

Should he open the door?

If she said yes, for all practical purposes the commitment to work through the betrothal process and arrive at a fully functioning marriage was made at that moment. Therefore, hers was not a lightly made decision, for the issue was not, "Can we have a wedding?" Once the door was opened the only remaining question was, "We can have a marriage if we can work out the terms . . . so what will they be?"

In other words, opening the door was the first major step toward making a marriage, which is precisely what Yeshua is saying in the above verse. You open the door, He comes in, and the restoration process begins. At that point you have salvation. But beyond that, He is asking you if you will enter into the covenant of betrothal with Him. Will you walk in a loving relationship with your bridegroom?

But that's not the only significant parallel here. The choice is "ours" exactly as the choice was always that of the ancient Hebrew bride. If she refused to open the door the groom would make a U-turn and head for home. And even after the bride opened the door she could end the whole process at any stage. In fact, once the initial agreement to be married was "darashed out" (i.e., worked out through intense, animated discussion) and formalized in a written contract, *the bride was the only one who could still back out, right up to the very instant of marriage consummation.* She could stop the whole process at any moment, and she didn't even need any special reason!

At the same time, once his initial proposal had been made and accepted, the groom was utterly and totally committed. Only by a writ of divorce, on extremely limited grounds, could he ever back out.

Differences and similarities

Again I invite you to compare the above to the betrothal covenant between ourselves and Yeshua. Opening the door is the same as accepting Him as our redeemer and forming a lasting relationship. It's the first step in the process.

On the other hand, we can accept eternal salvation and even avail ourselves of all the benefits of a servant covenant with Him without ever moving beyond that. In fact, if we decide to go further than simply opening the door, we might even be able to establish and maintain the servant covenant, then the friendship covenant, and perhaps even the inheritance covenant .

Becoming the actual bride of Yeshua requires a committed, intimate relationship with Him that goes well beyond all the preliminaries. How many of us are willing to separate or distance ourselves from those things of this world that are not pleasing to God?

Even so, if we do desire to take the betrothal step we can still back out at any time, and many of us do. Yet the invitation to be part of the bride is always there, except for those times when we give back the free gift of salvation.

As it says in II Timothy 2:11–13 (NIV):

> If we died with him, we will also live with him; if we endure, we will also reign with him. If we disown him, he will also disown us; if we are faithless, he will remain faithful, for he cannot disown himself.

The four cups of wine

Think once again in terms of the four types of covenant. Remember that they are progressive in nature, meaning that you must enter into the first three covenants, *in order*, before you can enter into number four. Remember also the names and the implications of each one, for you're about to see how the servant, friendship, and inheritance covenants are woven into covenant number four. Each one helps to establish, to support, and to reinforce the ancient Hebrew betrothal contract. In turn, the progression of commitments about to take place during the betrothal process, beginning on the evening when the groom comes and knocks, mirrors the sequence of commitments in the four covenants.

In his capacity as the Ultimate Master of Symbolism, God established four cups of wine as milestones, or "markers," to signify exactly where the betrothal parties were in their negotiations. Each cup corresponded to a covenant, but it also represented something that all the participants had to physically grasp, to physically consume and make part of themselves. It goes without saying that each person would also have to participate mentally and spiritually at each step of the way, or the process would break down.

Now, refer back to the reference to "sup with him" from Revelation 3:20, for it has to do with what traditionally happened next. Once the prospective groom and his father were inside the prospective bride's home, as they worked out all the details of the wedding they would eat dinner together with her family. In this instance, the visiting father and son represented their entire family.

Members of the two families would also drink three of the four betrothal cups of wine, one cup each at certain well-established points throughout the negotiating process.

Cup number one

The first cup was the Cup of Sanctification,[1] which equated to a servant (blood) covenant between the two families. This cup was consumed almost as soon as the door was closed. The groom, his father, and every member of the bride's family above the age of accountability participated, for each member of each family was agreeing to serve the other family.

Sanctification embodies the idea of setting ourselves apart for God. Just as God sanctified the nation of Israel, these two families were doing the same with respect to each other. In effect they were making a sacred commitment to become one giant family, each person to unilaterally serve all the new members. That's partly why the support structure underlying ancient Jewish marriages was so strong.

Cup number two

The second cup was the Cup of Betrothal, Cup of Plagues,[2] Cup of Bargaining, or the cup of Dedication, which represented a salt covenant between the families. This cup was consumed by the bride and groom and their two fathers only. The two families, represented here by the fathers, were covenanting to become eternal friends with their joint son and daughter, and with each other.

As they ate, the members of both families haggled over the details of the marriage contract (see *What is a ketubah?* below). This is usually where the negotiations would break down if they were ever going to. But if they managed to surmount all the difficulties, the families entered into a friendship covenant even as they established the terms of the upcoming marriage. In similar fashion, we are admonished to " . . . work out your salvation with fear and trembling" (Philippians 2:12) when we accept the Lord's offer of servanthood, which then matures into friendship.

The issues the families established were straightforward and direct, just as the ancient Hebrews themselves were. How much would the groom's family contribute to the wedding feast? Where would they hold it? What skills would the bride need to acquire to become a Proverbs 31 wife, an "excellent wife . . . her worth is far above jewels." (See Proverbs 31:10–31 for the complete description!)

What possessions would she bring with her? Did she fully understand her responsibility to remain pure?

The bride's family would also want to know how the groom intended to support her. Just as it was the bride's primary responsibility to purify and prepare herself, the groom's chief responsibility was to go away and prepare a place for her to live. Many times her new quarters would be no more than a room, built on the side of his father's house. This would hardly equal what Yeshua promises us in John 14:2, yet the whole process certainly corresponds to the reference in that verse in which Yeshua says, "In my Father's house are many mansions: if it were not so, I would have told you. I go to prepare a place for you." (KJV)

As His Father did before Him in the Old Testament, Yeshua often referred to Himself as a Bridegroom. The verse above is just one of many, demonstrating how He often spoke to His people via the ancient Hebrew marriage metaphor.[3]

A little digression

Before we go on to the third cup, let us deal with another side issue that often crops up. When we teach classes on the above subjects, somewhere near this point in our discussion of the Jewish betrothal covenant, someone always accuses us of promoting a "Doctrine of Works." So let us be clear.

We are not advocating any such thing. We are simply pointing out how the sacred betrothal system works, a system set up by God Himself to reclaim the bride who divorced Him back in the Garden of Eden. To review that system in the light of what we've talked about so far, *salvation* occurs when you open the door of your heart and ask the Savior to come in. The first reciprocal commitment you can then make, to further develop your relationship with God, occurs when you drink the first cup of wine. But you don't have to drink *any* cups – or perform *any* "works" – to be saved!

As we said nearer the beginning of this chapter, salvation equals . . . salvation! Nothing less, but also nothing more. Salvation requires repentance and acceptance; nothing more but also nothing less. "Works" aren't even in the picture, so get that thought out of your mind right now!

However, as Yeshua also made quite clear in the seventh chapter of Matthew, we *will* be *known* by our fruits. Not *justified*, but *known*. If we love Him we will obey Him, and if obeying Him means that certain works will manifest themselves in our lives, then so be it. Perhaps we'll start preparing food baskets for the poor. Maybe we'll begin tithing, or mowing the church lawn, or transporting the elderly on shopping trips.

But again, any such actions or activities that result from our love of Yeshua, and our commitment to following Him and doing the things that please Him, are not "works" undertaken to gain salvation. They are "fruits" that appear as a direct result of the Holy Spirit's indwelling within us and blossoming forth, and our decision to walk in obedience and relationship, through covenant.

As a bride who loves her husband might care for his parents or loan a dish to his sister, so we might do good things for the members of our groom's family – and for others as well. But in the bride's case, those "good works" are simply the logical results of her decision to love her groom.

So it is with us. The fruit of the tree should not be confused with the seed, the water, and the sunshine that brought it forth.

Going sideways again

While we're at it, let's look at another concept. In hammering out a betrothal covenant, ancient Hebrew families often wrestled with each other just like Jacob wrestled with God. Within their culture a certain amount of table-pounding and voice-raising was absolutely normal. Every family did it; if you weren't willing to stiffen your neck and defend your beliefs, what good were you?

God is the same way. He clearly responds to those who come to Him boldly but honorably. Think of the concessions He made for Sodom and Gomorrah at Abraham's request; the blessing he bestowed on Jacob who wouldn't surrender without one; the day He made the sun stand still when Joshua asked for more time to whip the Amorites before dark.

But think also of the moment when Moses pressed the Lord one too many times on the "Why can't I see Canaan?" question, and God told him to stop arguing and not mention the issue again. God has a lot of patience, but he also has an infinite memory.

Again, God is not automatically offended by interaction; not even by disagreement! We're talking about *relationships* here, which some-times require very spirited dialogue that flows in *two directions*.

When "negotiations" turn into outright defiance you know you're on thin ice, which is what happened to Moses in the ex-ample above. But until that point God is perfectly willing to listen to your objections. Sometimes He'll even modify His game plan, as long as wrestling doesn't turn into rebellion.

Cup number three

Coming back now to our sequence of cups, the third cup was the Cup of Redemption,[4] or the Cup of Inheritance, which represented a sandal covenant and signified the shared inheritance of the mar-riage partners. This cup was drunk at the end of the meal, by the bride and groom only, to symbolize their exclusive commitment to each other, along with their increasing level of intimacy.

It also officially "sealed" the marriage agreement between them. Once the bargaining was over the families brought in a scribe, who wrote out all the terms of the marriage covenant in a formal agreement, called a *ketubah* (again, see below). Probably the scribe, knowing that he was about to be called on, had most of the "boilerplate" (e.g., the histories of the bride and groom's families, and perhaps even some of the stipulations) written out in advance. Beyond that he simply added the specifics of each situation.

At that point the young men of the family would hit the streets and blow their ram's horn trumpets (*shofars*), announcing to all the world that the marriage contract had been signed. For all intents and purposes the bride and groom were now officially married, even though neither the ceremony nor the consummation had yet occurred. Nevertheless, from that moment onward, if either one died the survivor would fully inherit the deceased partner's possessions.

We can see the same dynamic at work as early as Genesis 19:14, when the angels warned Abraham's nephew, Lot, to leave Sodom before it was destroyed.

> Lot went out and spoke to his sons-in-law, who were to marry his daughters, and said, "Up, get out of this place, for the LORD will destroy the city." But he appeared to his sons-in-law to be jesting.

Our point is not that these young men failed to take him seriously. Rather, they were called his sons-in-law even though the official marriages had not yet taken place.

Sacred parallels

The third cup also corresponded to the cup Yeshua shared with His disciples during the Passover feast, or the Last Supper, when He washed their feet and thus transferred His inheritance to them (sandal covenant). He also made further reference to His coming marriage to His *kalah*, His "called out ones," knowing that it was customary for the groom not to drink wine again until the wedding ceremony. That explains why He said he would not touch the fruit of the vine again until He could do so with them in the Kingdom of Heaven. He even maintained this vow as He hung on the cross, when He refused the pain-numbing wine that the Roman soldiers offered.

Each time we take communion we should remember that we are literally reaffirming our commitment to be Yeshua's bride. This is always true at weddings and the Passover, for these are parallel celebrations in which God appears to be emphasizing – and then *re*-emphasizing – the sanctity and the intimacy of both our earthly unions with each other and our heavenly union with Him.

Indeed, the communion in the Upper Room is a picture of the covenant sequence, except that Yeshua reversed it! First He removed his disciples' sandals and washed their feet (inheritance). Next, He broke bread (friendship) and passed a cup of wine (service). Finally, He then went on to shed His blood on the Cross a few hours later, in the ultimate blood covenant.

In view of all this, when we take communion we also need to recognize, every single time, what He did on the cross. But it's equally important to remember that we're making a re-commitment to pursue Him; to wrestle with Him; to be His friend and manage His estate. When we take the cup we are committing again to serve Him, to obey Him, to follow His rules and ordinances, for the commitment we make at communion is the same as what a bride and groom make to each other.

None of this can be modified by our opinion or interpretation. We don't get a list of options, except for choosing whether we'll participate in the first place! Even in modern America, in a culture that barely honors covenants of any kind, if a man gives a woman a ring and proposes marriage, she doesn't accept his offer but then say, later on, "You intended this to mean that we would be married, but I intended it to mean that I'd marry your brother!"

Once we're in covenant with Yeshua we don't get the option of restructuring that relationship to suit ourselves. Yet sadly, the modern church has altered the very fabric of the Hebraic relationship that God began with Adam and Eve. We have literally thrown away our understanding in favor of "doing it our own way." We're too used to being Americans and believing we don't have to do things by any means other than what we, ourselves, choose!

Yet God has shown us very clearly how He wants to be approached. It's not our option to say that we, on the contrary, have a better idea. God says, "This is how you go about mending and restoring your relationship with Me. No other way will work."

Given that dynamic, it's totally presumptuous (and futile) of us to try to alter our relationship and our approach to God. From God's perspective, neither is the meaning and import of any of the four covenant types up for discussion. God offered mankind a betrothal contract starting 6,000 years ago, and sealed the terms 2,000 years ago. It's also not accidental that the cups of wine of the betrothal covenant overlay (and thus reinforce) the individual covenants in the sequence. All this happens on purpose, for God was building a *seamless mosaic of concepts* that has, at its foundation, a commitment to establish and maintain a relationship leading to marriage. And this is the ultimate responsibility. Hence it requires the ultimate covenant.

One other point

Taking all this lightly would be a big mistake. Paul said so himself, in 1 Corinthians 11:27–30. These things were not and are not "empty rituals." Their value resides in the obedience they bring about. We can't participate flippantly; we can't violate the betrothal covenant with God and not pay the price.

Another related point. It isn't necessary (and for most of us probably isn't even posssible) to commit to each of the four covenant types in one swift moment of glory. It takes time for God to work in our hearts, to reveal what He has in store and what He demands in return. Again, the covenants are progressive. To use a very simple analogy, in baseball you can't go straight to third base without going to first and second *in progression*. But it is our job to be listening when God calls us into more intimacy.

In other words, if you've allowed Yeshua to knock at your door and have invited Him inside, in the days that follow you may be anywhere from grasping the doorknob to drinking the third cup. Wherever you are, as long as you remain committed you're in exactly the right place. Just realize that, since you let Him in, you're *saved*. God will *ask* you (not *tell* you) to make additional moves toward greater intimacy with Him, but they'll come at His timing, as you conform to His will. The whole process starts with the fundamental servant covenant and moves forward from there.

Meanwhile, don't reach for the moon or feel condemned because you're only at point A and not point Z. When God wants you to move, to "drink the next cup," He'll make it perfectly clear and you'll know when He calls you to it. If God is not calling you to manage his estate because you're still working on service issues, don't feel guilty. Don't compare yourself to other people; compare yourself to what God is requiring of *you*. Work on what God has put in front of you *today*.

It's only when you don't maintain whatever covenant you've committed to that you begin to lose ground and fall backward. In ancient times, the price for breaking the marriage covenant was death by hanging, stoning, the sword, or the fire. For us, none of those options might seem to apply. On the other hand, the eternal price could actually be much higher.

Cup number four

The fourth cup of wine was the Cup of Praise,[5] shared between the bride and groom only during the wedding ceremony itself. This fourth cup also awaits all those who are chosen to be the bride by Yeshua. It will be taken on the wedding day and will forever seal Yeshua's union with His beloved.

We become eligible for the fourth covenant only after we've met all the previous requirements by entering into the first three. The decisions to do so are ours alone. However, Yeshua chooses His own bride, to whom He promised the crown of life in Revelation 2:10:

> Do not fear what you are about to suffer. Behold, the devil is about to cast some of you into prison, so that you will be tested, and you will have tribulation for ten days. Be faithful until death, and I will give you the crown of life.

Again, that's why Yeshua said, in Matthew 22:14, "For many are called but few are chosen."

What is a ketubah?

Ketubah[6] is the Hebrew word for *marriage contract*. As indicated above, the terms of the contract were worked out between the two families during the meal they shared together. When both sides were satisfied they brought in a scribe or a rabbi to write the actual document itself, which had five parts.

1) First came a combined family history of the bride and groom, which included detailed family trees and anecdotes.
2) Second came a personal and family history of the bride, with a detailed family tree and anecdotes.
3) Third came a personal and family history of the groom, also with a family tree and anecdotes.
4) Fourth came the story of how the bride and groom met, with related anecdotes.
5) Fifth came a final section detailing both the bride's and the groom's responsibilities before and after the wedding.

Let us pause for another moment and look at some more significant parallels to the marriage contract itself, one from the beginning of Scripture and one from the very end.

We would not be the first researchers to point out that the first five books of the Bible correspond to the five parts of the ancient Hebrew ketubah.

1) *Genesis* provides the combined family history of the bride and groom.
2) *Exodus* gives the personal and family history of the bride.
3) *Leviticus* provides the history of God's "family," the Levites.
4) *Numbers* tells of God's love affair with His people in the wilderness and records His joys and sorrows as He reaches out to His bride.
5) *Deuteronomy* specifies the responsibilities that both bride and groom must fulfill.

So what are we saying? That the first five books of the Bible are written as a marriage contract between God and His people. We're not even talking "analogy" here – that's what they *are*!

When all these details and conditions of the coming marriage were recorded in writing, the ketubah required seven signatures, seven "seals." These came from the bride and groom, the two fathers, a scribe (or, in later times, a rabbi), and two witnesses.

In our opinion, in the Torah those seven signatures come from seven major players. Remember our covenant patriarchs, in the previous chapter? They play a very important role in this ketubah, this marriage contract. Figuratively, they become the signatories as follows:

- Adam and Noah were the two witnesses.
- Abraham, the father of many nations, was also father of the groom.
- Jacob was the father of the bride.
- Moses was the scribe (he wrote down the Torah as God dictated).
- David, often called God's beloved, was the bride.
- Yeshua, representing salvation, was the groom.

At the end of the Bible, in the book of Revelation, we encounter the whole concept of the "seven seals" once again, in a very big way. To some researchers the references seem mysterious and difficult to understand, but in reality they refer, directly, to a classic Hebrew marriage ketubah.

I go to prepare a place . . .

To continue the sequence of betrothal events, by the time the happy couple had drunk the third cup of wine, only three more "milestones" remained.

1) **First**, the groom had to pay the bride price (which he'd brought with him), equaling thirty pieces (shekels) of silver in Yeshua's time. It was 100 percent refundable if the bride turned out to be impure. This specific amount was also the price of a male bondservant (Exodus 21:32) and came to symbolize the redemption price of a bride (Leviticus 27:4).[7]

2) **Second**, the groom now had the sole responsibility to go and prepare a home (see the familiar "I go to prepare a place for you" in John 14:1–3) where he would live with his bride, which was often (but not necessarily) an extension on the home of his own father. The building and furnishing process itself could take a year or two, during which the bride and groom had very little direct contact with each other.

   In this enterprise the groom was under the ironclad rule of his father, who was the only person empowered to judge when the groom's bridal preparations (as per the ketubah) were sufficient and complete. Likewise, in Mark 13:32 Yeshua says, "But of that day or hour no one knows, not even the angels in heaven, nor the Son, but the Father alone."

3) **Third**, as the groom finalized his preparations he would let the word slip out that the wedding day was near. Meanwhile, the bride's family and friends would begin preparing for a feast. The bride and bridesmaids would buy enough oil to keep their lamps lit for at least two weeks. The bridesmaids' job was to watch for the groom's arrival. When they saw him coming for his bride, their lamps would show the way. They were also expected to warn the bride, a small but very important job (Matthew 25:1–13).

The groom could come anytime between 6 PM and midnight, on the second through the fourth day of the week. When he did so he had to see his bride's welcoming light in her window. If she let it burn out he would take that as a sign that she had either changed her mind or simply didn't care anymore, and he would turn away and leave her in darkness.

The wedding party

When the groom arrived, late in the evening, he would be accompanied by a crowd of groomsmen, all of whom he would have selected well in advance, usually while building a residence for his bride. All would be males, all were virgins, and all would have close relationships with him. Their job was to guard him and announce his coming by blowing trumpets.

Meanwhile, the bridesmaids would warn the bride that her suitor was coming – as if she couldn't tell for herself! As soon as they got there the group would whisk the bride away. At that point, her bridesmaids would hurry to the wedding site. There they would light it up with their lamps and make final preparations. Then, as soon as all was ready the groom would take his bride's hand and lead her to the celebration site.

Through the rest of the night the wedding couple and their attendants would celebrate, with roast lamb, freshly baked bread, and plenty of wine. They would also enjoy the music of flutes, lyres, harps, and cymbals. This special event would be for the bridal party alone. The wedding would be held on the next day, with guests and relatives coming from all over.

The mikveh

A few hours before dawn, the groom and his men would leave the bride with her bridesmaids. Her friends would lead her to the *mikveh*, a ceremonial bath where she would be bathed in running ("living") water.[8] As in every Hebrew mikveh, or baptism, she would bow forward into the oncoming stream, facing the source as an act of love and submission to God, the source of all life.

The ancient Hebrews knew full well where life came from. Therefore, by honoring God through the mikveh, by submitting and subjegating their lives to Him, they brought into play another major symbol of covenant and purification.

In fact, the parallels are striking, for just as there were four cups of wine in the betrothal process there were also four general types of mikveh. As shown in Table 3-1, you could mikveh into repentence, into a deeper dedication to God, into ministry, and into marriage. John the Baptist offered a mikveh into repentence; Yeshua offered the remaining three. His life, and His frequent admonitions to His disciples, all demonstrated that a servant of the kingdom, who has entered into all three covenants, ministers to servants, friends, and other sons and daughters. And the best way to do that was to serve them. Thus, one who does so will be the greatest.

Table 3-1: Covenants and Mikvehs

Covenant	Cups	Mikveh
Blood	Servant	Repentance
Salt	Friendship	Dedication
Sandal	Inheritance	Ministry
Marriage	Marriage	Marriage

Following the mikveh, the bride's attendants would anoint her with fragrant oils, and she would return home to rest for a few hours before the morning. As her wedding day dawned, the bride would return to the place of the previous night's festivities. There her groom would be waiting, wearing pure white garments woven with threads of gold, and fragrant with the scent of myrrh, cassia, and frankincense.

The chuppah

As he escorted her to the *chuppah*, a dome of bright crimson cloth, its color symbolizing their covering by a blood covenant, the groom would also be wearing a wreath of fresh myrtle and roses, thorns included, a symbol that their love would bring him both joy and pain (Does this sound familiar?). Somewhat earlier, a broad circlet of gold, shaped into the silhouette of the city of Jerusalem, would have been placed on the bride's head.

The couple would perform the wedding ceremony themselves, during which the groom would pronounce his bride pure, holy, and set apart for him alone. They would speak seven blessings over each other and vow their eternal faithfulness and love. After completing their vows they would share the fourth cup of wine together, the final step in the long betrothal process which began with the groom's proposal perhaps more than a year ago.

When they finished this fourth cup the groom would place it on the ground and put his foot on it. The bride would rest her foot on his and together they would stomp the cup to pieces, assuring that no one else would ever drink from it, thus signifying the exclusivity of their relationship.

Next the bride and groom would take a triple-braided loaf of *challah* bread, bless it, break it, dip it in salt, and feed it to each other as a further pledge of their friendship and a renewal of the salt covenant. Then the groom would give his bride a new inheritance by removing her old, worn-out sandals, washing her feet, and putting on a new pair. Both of these customs clearly reinforce the pillars of covenant, the foundation underlying ancient Hebrew marriages on which modern marriages as well should stand.

At that point the bride and groom would sometimes exchange rings, placing them on their right hands. The bride and groom were considered a king and queen for a week, starting with their wedding day. As the queen stands at the king's right hand, so the bride must always symbolically be at her groom's right hand.

Another digression . . .

Right here we'd like to insert a fuller explanation of one more extremely familiar verse. Matthew 23:37 says:

> "Jerusalem, Jerusalem, who kills the prophets and stones those who are sent to her! How often I wanted to gather your children together, the way a hen gathers her chicks under her wings, and you were unwilling."

Most of us understand this verse on the simplest level, as saying that He loved them and still loves us, as a mother hen loves her chicks. But from a Hebrew perspective this verse means much more. Remember, Hebrew scripture works on four levels! The Hebrew word translated as "wings" is *kanaf* and can mean wings, but here it is also used to describe the corners of Yeshua's prayer shawl, His talit. Hanging from the corners of the talit are the tzit-tzit, what most people call "fringes" but which are actually four cords doubled over and knotted in a distinct pattern, numerically spelling out the name of God.

Yeshua Himself provided the "hen" metaphor, but in addition He was referring to what a loving groom would do for his wife. At the end of a Hebrew marriage ceremony he would spread his arms around her and wrap her up in his talit, thus protecting her but also making them as one, even as he "covered" both of them with the name and the word of God.

Thus He was also saying how much he yearned to be in a marriage relationship with his people.

Yeshua, our kinsman redeemer

After the ceremony itself came the moment of yachid, or physical unity. The parents of the bride would invite the guests to enjoy the feast. The music would swell, the dancing would begin, and the wine would flow for the first of seven days.

Meanwhile, the bride and groom would slip away to a private room, set apart from the noise and provided especially for them. Soon their marriage would be complete in every sense.

On the other hand, if the groom discovered that his bride was not a virgin, (or, worse yet, discovered that she was already pregnant) the whole situation would immediately change. Within the ancient Hebrew culture, the groom had four choices:

1) He could let her pay the price for her unfaithfulness, which was death.

2) He could quietly give her a writ of divorce and walk away, which is what Joseph started to do with Mary before the angel intervened. But this approach was risky for her; later on, if other witnesses came forward to accuse her of adultery, the law would still require her to pay the death penalty (Matthew 1:19).

3) He could pretend that the child was his. If he discovered the truth before the wedding, he could forfeit the ceremony and simply begin living with his new wife, who was already married to him anyway from a legal point of view. This is essentially what Joseph did with Mary, although the trip to Bethlehem and the subsequent two-year sojourn in Egypt among strangers pretty much allowed the two of them to escape any immediate social fallout from what might have looked like the premature birth of Yeshua. This option, however, is not available to our Redeemer Bridegroom; our God requires that His son's bride be pure and holy.

4) He could choose to be her *goel* (redeemer)[9] and take her punishment upon himself. In the case of sexual impurity, he would pay her fee . . . death.

The groom could also redeem his bride for violating Torah in other ways as well, whatever her violations might involve, including monetary debts of all kinds. The biggest drawback in this approach was that the groom could never again refuse to pay for any "required redemption" as long as they stayed married. He'd established a potentially harsh precedent; once he'd redeemed her *even one time* he had to pay the same price every time she violated Torah after that, as long as she was his wife.

Now consider the scriptural parallels. Way back in the Garden of Eden, Yeshua was faced with a bride who had rejected Him. Yet He still made a commitment to pay her bridal price. He also began immediately the complicated process of remarrying humanity, starting with the first blood sacrifice (Genesis 3:21). Indeed, the Hebrew text describes the garments of skins that God provided Adam and Eve as *katanot*,[10] the first layer of the Hebrew bride's wedding attire.

In other words, God was clothing Adam and Even in bridal garments. "Here, I can solve this problem; will you take the first step in re-marrying me?" He said. He was also saying, "Will you accept me by serving and obeying my principles of restoration?" even as Adam and Eve saw the blood that was spilled and responded in the affirmative.

This was the first step in the process of wooing mankind back to the kind of ultimate relationship that God has wanted to have with us since we were created. Through covenant He chose to provide a means by which His bride could be healed and mended so her groom could see her as pure, not because she *was* pure but because He had *paid her price.*

Nevertheless, we still have an adversary who stands accusing us (Revelation 12:10), doing his best to pretend that we're unredeemed and thus demanding that payment be made for our sins. That payment is also death (Romans 6:23), but Yeshua has already chosen to ransom His bride with His own life (Matthew 26:38–42, Romans 5:8).

This is the divine romance that every believer can experience. From the beginning, God intended that mankind should be His bride. When that divine relationship was broken in the Garden of Eden, man effectively handed God a divorce. But Yeshua has long since paid the price and re-established the relationship, for those willing to partake.

What does all this mean?

With each chapter of this book we are gradually introducing the fundamental concepts that underlie B'rit Hadashah and the book of Revelation, to be covered in their entirety in the second volume in this series. When we begin working with Revelation, if you've kept up, you'll understand it as never before. For now, the message is still quite simple. Each of us has both the obligation and the privilege of choosing the relationship we will have with God. We can be His servant, His friend, His son, or His daughter.

Beyond that, we can purify ourselves, accept each of the covenants He offers, and accept the ultimate union. We can be part of His bride.

But becoming part of the bride doesn't happen automatically. This is probably the most important point of this whole chapter. Many Christians assume that salvation alone is all they need to become "one with Christ," now and forever united with Him as His Chosen One, His bride dressed in white.

It isn't that simple. Salvation equals . . . salvation! Nothing less, but also nothing more, to repeat a phrase we've used before. Salvation/covenant/betrothal is not a three-for-one sale. Salvation means you can come to the wedding, which is quite an invitation all by itself, but you can't be a guest and a bride at the same time.

To put it another way, you pay as you go, but oh — what a journey!

In summary . . .

- ◆ The Marriage Covenant is the culmination of the previous three covenants — servanthood, friendship, and inheritance. It's offered to all of us, but relatively few accept its privileges and responsibilities.
- ◆ The bride and groom take four cups to consummate this marriage, the last during the ceremony/wedding celebration itself.
- ◆ What is often called the *Torah*, meaning the first five books of the Bible, is written like a ketubah, an ancient Hebrew marriage contract.
- ◆ Yeshua has redeemed us exactly as an ancient Hebrew husband could redeem his sinful wife.
- ◆ Yeshua has already shared the first three cups of betrothal wine with His intended bride. Only one remains.

4

Devils and Demons

Back in the 1950s, a young comedian named Red Skelton hosted a radio show in which he supplied all the voices – and some of the sound effects as well – for a bunch of zany characters. One of those characters had somehow trapped the devil and locked him in his attic.

So, whenever the "Mean Little Kid" (pronounced "widdle") came on the show, listeners were treated to a lot of banging on an imaginary door, and a lot of hilarious repartee between an impotent devil and a savvy little smart aleck. The devil made a million promises but the kid always fended him off and kept the padlock in place, no matter how much he might have been tempted by one of the devil's alluring bribes.

Oh, that it might be that simple! If we could just lock the devil in the closet and throw away the key, mankind might be so much better off! But that, of course, is not what happens until the end (Rev. 20:10).

So who is this devil, anyway, and where does he come from?

Satanic origins

Much of the history of the monumental conflict between the evil spirit being we call *Satan*, and the God against whom he rebelled, is recorded in Scripture. But understanding the details requires a certain amount of independent study and cross-referencing. For that reason alone, some of the material we present below remains somewhat controversial.

Some scholars even refuse to consider anything at all that was not voted into the final biblical canon by the Catholic Church at the Council of Constantinople, in AD 553. This is especially true of the book of *Enoch,* a tremendously helpful text which often details with startling clarity the concepts that are not so easily understood in the traditional Scriptures. Enoch was considered "regular canon" in Yeshua's time. It was established and recognized as part of Torah, was quoted by several of the writers of both testaments,[1] but was thrown out by the Catholic Church for reasons that will soon become apparent.

The book of Enoch gives us incomparable insight into the difference between "devils" and "demons." That clear difference is one of those major, seldom understood concepts that reappear throughout Scripture but are almost never talked about in modern Christian churches. And yet, Yeshua clearly acknowledged it in Matthew 17:21 ("But this kind does not go out except by prayer and fasting") and Mark 9:29.

This understanding – of a definite difference between devils and demons – is many thousands of years old. In Yeshua's time it was a common understanding among the Jewish people, and among rabbis in particular. Hence He felt no need to over-explain Himself in the Scriptures cited above. It is still understood by Hebrew people today who are educated in such matters.

In fact, the notion that devils and demons are the same is the *newer* concept. It was arbitrarily introduced into the Christian Church in AD 553 by the Council of Constantinople, as noted above. The leaders of that convocation ruled that any written opinion that distinguished between devils and demons must be destroyed. Or, to be accepted by the Church it must be altered in line with the "new thinking."

This ruling was an expansion of the Anti-Jewish laws initiated in AD 327. It meant that *Mishnah, Talmud* (rabbinical commentaries on the Bible), and more ancient books, such as the book of *Enoch,* were immediately outlawed – but only because they couldn't be completely destroyed. Officially, the Roman Church claimed that those books no longer had any value in providing insight into Scripture, and they were even declared "heretical." Indeed, the same ruling *almost* succeeded in deleting the books of I and II Peter and Jude, because of their agreement with (and references to) the book of Enoch.

The council's change, from acceptance to rejection of the fundamental devils/demons distinction, was also a reaction against an influx of mystical, pagan, and heretical teaching by many of the early Greek church fathers, such as Origen and Tertullian. The truth of that distinction was thrown out because it too closely resembled some of the more bizarre teachings of these men. The Council excommunicated Origen, post-mortem, and condemned the previously accepted understanding regarding devils and demons. Mainly, the Roman Church was afraid that the uneducated masses would be unable to distinguish between heresy and a truth that involved what they felt were some very "strange and disturbing" elements.

In other words, only the elite (i.e., themselves) could handle such knowledge, so they simply decreed that it would no longer officially exist.

Too bad for them, because it's almost impossible to destroy all traces of such an important truth. Therefore, let us transport ourselves to a moment much closer to the beginning of our world. In the process, let us fill in some of the details so we can all understand the "who and what" we're dealing with now, thousands of years later, when we speak of Satan, devils, and demons.

A very clear distinction

The ancient Hebrew language used different words for devils and demons, which are utterly distinct and carry with them various characteristics attributed to each separate entity. One word for devil with which you are already familiar is *ha Satan*, Hebrew for "the adversary." He is also known as the "enemy" and the "accuser." Ha Satan is the source for the modern English word *Satan*, his most familiar designation.

Ironically, Satan *never was* his *name*! Ha Satan was a *title*, chosen by God and given to a cherub whose *real* name we *do not know*. When that cherub rebelled and was thrown out of heaven, God literally took away his identity by removing his name and giving him a title instead, thus conveying total dishonor.

In its regrettable "innocence" the Western church has erred grievously by turning a Hebrew description into a name, thus giving the honor of a personal name *back* to Ha Satan, the leader of the evil hordes. This is exactly the opposite of what God intended. We compound our error when we claim that he was also known, by God, as *Lucifer*, for this was a totally subjective name given to him by the Babylonians, based on the understanding that he comes as an angel of light.

In II Corinthians 11:13–15, Paul puts forth the same claim, along with a warning for us to watch out for false prophets who come in Satan's place:

> For such men are false apostles, deceitful workers, disguising themselves as apostles of Christ. No wonder, for even Satan disguises himself as an angel of light. Therefore it is not surprising if his servants also disguise themselves as servants of righteousness, whose end will be according to their deeds.

Note that Isaiah also seems to refer to him as Lucifer in the King James translation of Isaiah 14:12 (emphasis added, below). But that still doesn't mean that the Lord ever knew him by that name. Indeed, many biblical scholars consider this translation erroneous, and most translations now insert "morning star," "son of the dawn," or something similar:

> How art thou fallen from heaven, O *Lucifer*, son of the morning! how art thou cut down to the ground, which didst weaken the nations! (KJV)

Some alternate Hebrew terms for a devil are *baal* and *teraphim*. But *baal* actually means "lord" or "chieftain"; most often it's used more as a title than a name. For example, calling someone "Baal Harrington" in the ancient Hebrew language would be like saying "Lord Harrington" in English.

On the other hand, Elijah, the prophet of God, fought and destroyed the prophets of Baal (with a capital B) on Mt. Carmel (I Kings 18:18–40). Clearly, the prophets that Elijah destroyed were worshipping and serving devils, or fallen angels, of whom the chief was Baal.

The idea that devils had their own dedicated worshippers in the days of Elijah is substantiated further when you consider the possible meanings of the word *teraphim*, which we'll get to in a moment. But by way of preview, if you're a *fallen* teraphim, you want people to worship you. How would you get them to do that? By establishing an idol! All of which brings up an excellent rule of thumb. Whenever you encounter spiritual beings that are trying to get you to worship them, they are devils.

In the beginning . . .

If the above jungle of partial definitions seems confusing . . . well, that's not surprising! Let's clarify by going back to the very beginning. As we know, God created all things. But even before God created all the life forms on Earth He also created a huge host of heavenly beings, commonly called *angels*. They were dedicated to eternal service to Him. In a sense, from their moment of creation they have been God's hands and feet, for they are the ones who carry out many of His missions throughout His creation.

But not all angels are equal, for Scripture tells us that God created three separate "orders," each one having a unique form, function, and purpose. In the Hebrew singular their titles were teraph, seraph, and cherub. The Hebrew plural forms are as follows.

    1) The *cherubim*,[2] also called *archangels*, are angels of the highest and the most powerful order. They literally surround the throne of God. Cherubim have six wings, four faces, and are quite large. The four faces (Revelation 4:7, Ezekiel 1:10) are a man's face, a lion's face, a bull's face, and an eagle's face. They are also covered with eyes.

We are introduced in the Bible to four cherubim. The most commonly known are the Archangel Michael (the Prince of Israel), the Archangel Gabriel, and the two who fell, one called "Lucifer" in the King James Version of Isaiah 14:12 as discussed several paragraphs previously, and one called Abaddon, now the angel of Death (see below). The other two, Uriel and Raphael, are referred to in extra-biblical writings – the Talmud, Mishnah, and apocryphal books.

Here are the meanings of the names of the four cherubim/archangels who did not rebel and thereby kept their positions before the throne of God:

- **Michael**   Warrior (prince) of God
- **Gabriel**   Redeemer of God
- **Raphael**   Healer of God; bringer of God's Healing
- **Uriel**   Light of God; bringer of God's Light

All these names end with "el," which is a Hebrew word (or suffix) meaning *God*. Each of these four angels represents some attribute, characteristic, or service that originates with God.

Two of the original cherubim, one-third of the original six, rebelled against God. The four named above remained true to God, while the one we (probably mistakenly) call Lucifer (again, the one who often comes as a Cherub of Light) and Abaddon (originally the Cherub of Life, who was also the foundation of the throne and is now the Cherub of Death) both fell. Lucifer's downfall is indelibly recorded in Ezekiel 28:13–19:

[13]You were in Eden, the garden of God; every precious stone was your covering: The ruby, the topaz and the diamond; the beryl, the onyx and the jasper; the lapis lazuli, the turquoise and the emerald; and the gold, the workmanship of your settings and sockets, was in you. On the day that you were created they were prepared.

[14]You were the anointed cherub who covers, and I placed you there. You were on the holy mountain of God; you walked in the midst of the stones of fire. [15]You were blameless in your ways from the day you were created until unrighteousness was found in you. [16]By the abundance of your trade you were internally filled with violence, and you sinned; therefore I have cast you as profane from the mountain of God. And I have destroyed you, O covering cherub, from the midst of the stones of fire.

[17]Your heart was lifted up because of your beauty; you corrupted your wisdom by reason of your splendor. I cast you to the ground; I put you before kings, that they may see you. [18]By the multitude of your iniquities, in the unrighteousness of your trade you profaned your sanctuaries. Therefore I have brought fire from the midst of you; it has consumed you, and I have turned you to ashes on the earth in the eyes of all who see you. [19]All who know you among the peoples are appalled at you; you have become terrified and you will cease to be forever.

In the King James Version, verse 16 says:

> By the multitude of thy merchandise they have filled the midst of thee with violence, and thou hast sinned: therefore I will cast thee as profane out of the mountain of God: and I will destroy thee, *O covering cherub,* from the midst of the stones of fire. (Italics added)

This reference to the "covering cherub" could also refer to covenant, which is sometimes referred to as a "covering" and is directly related to the chuppah, the literal covering so central to the ancient Hebrew wedding ceremony as we explained in the previous chapter.

In any case, God stripped both Lucifer and Abaddon of their original names and their positions of authority. *Note that this development further reinforces our understanding that Hebrew names embody identity.* However, as we have indicated several times already, the evil being we now call Satan can appear as an angel of light because he's a deceiver. Hence, even though God took his name away he is still sometimes known as *Lucifer,* which is a Babylonian variant of *Lucent* from Latin, meaning "light," and is the name we referenced in Isaiah 14:12 several pages back.

2) The *seraphim*[3] are the middle order of angels and are sometimes known as "Burning Ones" or "Healing Angels." According to scripture these angels burn with fire and, like the cherubim, are covered with eyes. As messengers of God they race back and forth between heaven and Earth, doing His will. By way of illustration, the ancient Hebrew word in Revelation 8:7 (*seraph*) that is commonly translated as "fire" raining down on the earth also refers to seraphim coming down from heaven as "heavenly fire." A Hebrew word more commonly used to refer to natural fire only would be *esh.*

Much earlier in the Bible, in telling the story of Jacob's ladder, Genesis 28:12 says:

> He had a dream, and behold, a ladder was set on the earth with its top reaching to heaven; and behold, the angels of God were ascending and descending on it.

In this passage, the original Hebrew suggests that what Jacob saw were seraphim, or messengers of God.

3) The *teraphim*[4] are the lowest order of angels. They are the only ones who can take on human form and maintain it for extended periods. You may even entertain them unaware, as indicated in Hebrews 13:2:

> Do not neglect to show hospitality to strangers, for by this some have entertained angels without knowing it.

In addition, *teraphim* are also denoted by the Hebrew word *ayir*,[5] which means "watcher." Daniel 4:10,17,18 refers to angels that watch over us and serve as protecters and custodians of men's souls. Truly, these are our guardian angels. So the television show "Touched by an Angel" is accurate in that sense; it refers to teraphim. Likewise, though he probably did not make any such distinction in his own mind, Michael Landon played a teraphim in the *Highway to Heaven* television series.

When they are fallen, teraphim are also called "idols," as in the NASB translation of Genesis 31:34:

> Now Rachel had taken the household idols and put them in the camel's saddle, and she sat on them. And Laban searched through all the tent but did not find them.

Most other familiar translations of this passage use the word "images." The Hebrew word from which "idols" or "images" comes (*ha teraphim*) indicates that the spirits behind the wooden idols (carved figures) that Rachel stole from her father's household were fallen teraphim.

Please note that there is no illusion of power involved here at all. Such evil power comes from the fallen angels, or devils, who are literally the power behind each idol. This is why many such false gods are "real" in a literal sense, even in the modern era, especially the highly worshipped gods of black magic sects.

To bring this into a modern context, in the movie *City of Angels*, starring Nicholas Cage and Meg Ryan, the guys in black were actually fallen teraphim. Along with all their cohorts several thousand years earlier, they were put into the abyss pending their eventual emergence as detailed in the book of Enoch and referenced in both Jude and II Peter.

> And angels who did not keep their own domain, but abandoned their proper abode, He has kept in eternal bonds under darkness for the judgment of the great day. (Jude 6)

> For if God did not spare angels when they sinned, but cast them into hell and committed them to pits of darkness, reserved for judgment... (II Peter 2:4)

In the movie the teraphim loved the sun. The movie didn't say it, but could this be true because they'd been in darkness for 5,000 years? Again, whether its makers know it or not, in many ways this movie is really an amazingly accurate takeoff on Genesis 6 and the book of Enoch.

Fallen watchers — the real, living beings on which the fictional versions above are based – are called *sayir*. Greek mythology refers to satyrs who are half-man, half-beast. Could this be a reference to the Hebrew word *sayir*? The books of Jude and II Peter both speak of angels who did not keep their positions of authority and are bound in chains, in darkness, awaiting judgment. In all these cases, the Hebrew word used for these angels is *sayir*, whose pictographic meaning is "watches to destroy [consume] men's souls." These words perfectly describe devils.

The ultimate devil

When the once-righteous creature known to Isaiah as Lucifer (the once-trusted archangel whom we will call *Satan* from here on, in deference to his most common "name") rebelled against God, he set in motion a far-reaching sequence of events much more profound than the simplified version most of us know so well today.

For example, it's certainly a possibility, that, when Satan and his hordes were thrown out of heaven, Satan took with him one-third of each group of angels – that is, one-third of the cherubim, one-third of the seraphim, and one-third of the teraphim. The Bible does not make this explicit (although, as mentioned above, Satan clearly took with him one-third of the original six cherubim), even in the original Hebrew, but all signs indicate that Satan's "third of the angels" was evenly distributed across the three types.

Genesis 3:1–19 tells how Satan took center stage in the familiar story of the Fall of Man, which occurred sometime after Satan's own downfall. Soon after God created Adam and Eve, Satan looked down upon them with jealousy. How dare this frail, dull creature be given the authority and dominion that could just as well have been his?! So Satan led the assault upon the first man and woman. Taking the guise of an earthly creature, he tricked man into trading his covenant relationship with God for the false concept of *equality* with God.

Satan operated according to the old "Sell the sizzle, not the steak!" adage, which probably wasn't old at all when he whipped it out. No one knows for sure what Adam and Eve were thinking, but it's hard to believe they would expect to achieve "equality with God," for that was impossible and they knew it. On the contrary, we believe they might have felt that "knowledge," as represented by the fruit from the tree, might make them even better companions of God. Perhaps they thought it might somehow enhance their relationship by narrowing the knowledge gulf between them and their Creator.

Instead, they fell for a sales pitch and lost almost everything, and *the price that man had to pay, from that day forward, has been beyond comparison.* Now, death had the ultimate dominion. Man lost his immortality, lost out on paradise, was driven from the presence of God, and was doomed to toil in pain and futility from that time on. But this was not the end of the story – not by a long shot.

In His anger, and the overwhelming sense of betrayal He must have felt (for the Lord has the original emotions that ours are based on), God said to the serpent, "And I will put enmity between you and the woman, and between your seed and her seed; he shall bruise you on the head, and you shall bruise him on the heel" (Genesis 3:15).

One widely held interpretation holds that the above verse is the first scriptural reference to the coming of Messiah. But even though this is partially true, we still need to dig a little deeper. Some have called the whole story nothing more than a fascinating myth, invented to explain why snakes crawl on their bellies. But what is actually being revealed in the Hebrew text is much more sinister.

Most translations use the word "they" rather than "he" to identify who is doing the bruising and treading. But as translated in the NASB, when God says to Satan, "And I will put enmity between you and the woman, And between your seed and her seed; He shall bruise you on the head, And you shall bruise him on the heel," (Genesis 3:15) God is literally making a prophecy about two sets of offspring, Satan's and man's. The Hebrew word *zarah*, referring to Satan's offspring, is the same Hebrew word used for Adam and Eve's offspring. But we're not talking about *spiritual* descendents; the Hebrew word means blood relatives, or *physical* descendants.

In other words, Satan has kids and mankind has kids in exactly the same context. His kids and your kids are equally real in a physical sense.

Satan was not satisfied with the partial victory he'd won. He immediately implemented a scheme that spanned throughout time and called for nothing less than the complete assimilation of man into Satan's own unholy legions.

Enter the nephilim

What came next is a horror to even contemplate, a monstrous "If you can't beat 'em, join 'em!" plot that looked at one point as if it might succeed. The sixth chapter of Genesis gives a few of the details; *The Book of Enoch*, quoted below, tells the rest of the story. A group of 200 of Satan's fallen angels (teraphim), led by one named *Samyaza*, made a pact whereby they took on human form, seduced the daughters of men, and produced giant offspring, a hybrid of devils and humans called *nephilim*.[6] One of these creatures, in the singular, would be a *nephal*.

Remember, as indicated in Genesis 6:2, teraphim can take on fleshly form for extended periods of time. And yes, to put it bluntly one more time, they *did* have sexual relations with human woman, called *sirens*. And they *did* produce *offspring* that were *not* created by God.

Now, to further understand what we're saying here, recall what we said in chapter one about the way Hebrew words are formed, with internal meanings of their own embodied within each of the letters (e.g., "Shalom" means "peace" in English, but pictographically, internally, it means "destroy the authority that binds us to chaos"). In that context, certain letters of the Hebrew aleph-bet make a clear distinction between various kinds of "life," especially between animal life and human life.

In general, the Hebrew word *chai* means "life," but *chai* can be spelled in three different ways, with each spelling referring to a distinct type of life.

1) The first way to spell chai, as shown in Table 4-1, uses the Hebrew characters *chet-yod-yod*. Pictographically, this is a picture of God putting a fence (chet) around His work

(yod). This fence of protection encloses God's orderly creation and prevents chaos from entering. Biologically speaking, without these fences of protection, life cannot last very long; for example, the cell wall or the skin that covers our bodies provides irreplaceable protection.

The first yod, pictographically, represents the work of God. The second yod explains how He made it, by forming it with His own hand and breathing life into it. In this creation passage, God was revealing the nature of the unique and intimate relationship He was proposing to have with mankind. He was further affirming that man is separate and distinct from all other kinds of life, made by God's hand in His own image, with his life literally "breathed in" by God. This word also correlates to (i.e., symbolically signifies) the Hebrew word, *nishmah*, which ancient rabbis spoke about as representing the spark of God that dwells within each human.

2) The second way of spelling chai uses the Hebrew characters *chet-yod*, which references the Hebrew word "nefash." Nefash means "all other life that God spoke forth." This stands in contrast to the only form of life that He literally formed with His own hands. This spelling can be used for all life of any kind, including man and animals. It refers to all life in existence – everything that's alive. The one yod represents the work that God did in making this kind of life . . . He spoke it forth and put a fence of protection around it as well.

3) The third way to spell chai uses only the Hebrew letter *chet*. This spelling contains no *yod* (work of God) at all, meaning that both God's work and His spirit are completely absent from it. Yet oddly enough, it still designates "a living thing." This usage of chet is limited to nephilim only, but has sometimes been translated as "evil beast," presumably to avoid confusion with a "wild beast" such as a lion or bear.

Table 4-1: Chai, or "life"

Spelling	Pictographic Symbols	Word	Meaning
Chet-yod-yod (Symbolizes protection for the work of God's hands)	A fence of protection around the work of God's hands	Chai	God-breathed life, produced by the hand of God — mankind only
Chet-yod (Symbolizes protection for work of God)	A fence of protection around God's work	Chai	All life, including mankind
Chet (Symbolizes protection)	A fence of protection	Chai	Nephilim, or "evil beasts"

God always uses a chet to "fence off" and separate His work from chaos. At the same time, man is the only thing God made – literally – with His own hands. All the rest of creation came from His speaking the words to make it emerge from nothingness. But to make man He used the personal touch, forming man with His own hand before He breathed life into his nostrils.

What a difference between man and nephilim! Nevertheless, in our modern translations of Scripture the truth still isn't always clear. When the Bible talks about nephilim they are usually called the offspring of sexual union between "sons of God" and daughters of earth." And with respect to what happened next . . . well, in the King James version, Genesis 6:12 is rendered:

> And God looked upon the earth, and, behold, it was corrupt; for all flesh had corrupted his way upon the earth.

Unfortunately, the King James translators chose to use the generic words "corrupt" and "corrupted," rather than indicating clearly that the "evil beasts" – the nephilim – were responsible for what actually took place.

Fortunately, in *Gesenius' Hebrew-Chaldee Lexicon to the Old Testament*[7] the word *nephilim* is defined as "a living abortion," or "to fall to the ground from heaven," or "to become a ruin." So the truth isn't completely hidden from those who search.

Finally, here's one more very revealing distinction. The Hebrew letters for the word *nephal* are *nun-pay-lamed*, which pictographically means "to speak control over life." God doesn't do this; on the contrary, He's into speaking *freedom*. God's purpose, through covenant, is the opposite of Satan's. In other words, this satanic strategy of interbreeding between man and devils represents Satan's attempt at controlling mankind for his own purposes. Since the moment they were first conceived the nephilim have been trying to control mankind, which is exactly the opposite of what God would do.

Nephilim in the headlights

For many years, all over the globe, in studying almost every ancient civilization, researchers have uncovered remarkably similar myths about the flood and the creation. Often these myths include very specific details that corroborate the Genesis account. For example:

> One flood account from the Tehuelche of Patagonia includes this comment in regards to the reason why God brought on the flood: "At a remote time in the past, the earth was inhabited also by people other than those created by the sun god. They were very bad and fought among themselves all the time. When the sun god saw this, he decided to annihilate these people and to create another population in their stead. To destroy the bad people the sun god sent torrential and continuous rain, the springs opened, and the ocean overflowed."

Obviously, these people worshipped the sun God as their creator god, but the story is still the same. Yet where did these people get the idea that there were "men" living on the earth that were not created by their God?[8]

The Tanakh, the Holy Scriptures (i.e., the Old Testament), published by the Jewish Publication Society,[9] translates Genesis 6:1-2 into English as:

> When men began to increase on earth, and daughters were born to them, the divine beings saw how beautiful the daughters of men were and took wives from among those that pleased them.

Chapters 7 and 8 of the book of Enoch give us a much clearer look at the details of the story told in Genesis 6. Enoch explains that the guys who show up on Earth and cohabit with the daughters of men were not the "sons of God" at all, as claimed in Genesis 6:2,4 in the King James translation, and several other translations as well – or as the "divine beings" in the Jewish Publication Society translation of verses one and two directly above. Rather, Enoch calls them "sons of heaven," which makes a lot more sense considering their source.

The following passage from Enoch is somewhat long, but given its importance (and the difficulty some readers might have in acquiring the text for themselves) we are including both chapters seven and eight in their entirety.

The Book of Enoch, Chapter 7 (Section 2)

> [1]It happened after the sons of men [Ed. Note: "normal" humans] multiplied in those days, that daughters were born to them, elegant and beautiful. [2]And when the angels, the ***sons of heaven*** [Ed.

93

Note: boldface Italics added], beheld them, they became enamoured of them, saying to each other, come, let us select for ourselves wives from the progeny of men, and let us beget children.

³Then their leader Samyaza said to them; I fear that you may perhaps be indisposed to the performance of this enterprise;

⁴And that I alone shall suffer for so grievous a crime.

⁵But they answered him and said; We all swear;

⁶And bind ourselves by mutual execration, that we will not change our intention, but execute our projected undertaking.

⁷Then they swore all together, and all bound themselves by mutual execrations. Their whole number was two hundred, who descended upon Ardis, which is the top of mount Armon.

⁸That mountain therefore was called Armon, because they had sworn upon it, and bound themselves by mutual execrations.

⁹These are the names of their chiefs: Samyaza, who was their leader, Urakabarameel, Akibeel, Tamiel, Ramuel, Danel, Azkeel, Saraknyal, Asael, Armers, Batral, Anane, Zavebe, Samsaveel, Ertael, Turel, Yomyael, Arazyal. These were the prefects of the two hundred angels, and the remainder were all with them.

¹⁰Then they took wives, each choosing for himself; whom they began to approach, and with whom they cohabited; teaching them sorcery, incantations, and the dividing of roots and trees.

¹¹And the women conceiving brought forth giants,

¹²Whose stature was each three hundred cubits. These devoured all *which* the labour of men *produced*; until it became impossible to feed them;

[13]When they turned themselves against men, in order to devour them;

[14]And began to injure birds, beasts, reptiles, and fishes, to eat their flesh one after another, and to drink their blood.

[15]Then the earth reproved the unrighteous.[10]

The Book of Enoch, Chapter 8

[1]Moreover, Azazyel taught men to make swords, knives, shields, breastplates, the fabrication of mirrors [made them see that which was behind them], and the workmanship of bracelets and ornaments, the use of paint, the beautifying of the eyebrows, *the use of* stones of every valuable and select kind, and of all sorts of dyes, so that the world became altered.

[2]Impiety increased; fornication multiplied; and they transgressed and corrupted all their ways.

[3]Amazarak taught all the sorcerers, and dividers of roots:

[4]Armers *taught* the solution of sorcery;

[5]Barkayal *taught* the observers of the stars;

[6]Akibeel *taught* signs;

[7]Tamiel taught astronomy;

[8]And Asaradel taught the motion of the moon.

[9]And men, being destroyed, cried out; and their voice reached to heaven.

Chapters 9–11 of Enoch detail God's response to what the fallen "sons of heaven" had done. We highly recommend these passages (the entire book of Enoch, for that matter!) for complete details of events that are only hinted at in other primary sources, including the Bible.

Basic definitions

The Bible tells us how Satan appeared in the Garden of Eden and tempted Adam and Eve to disobey God. Contrary to popular belief, man does not belong to the earth; the earth actually belongs to man. God gave us this planet to care for and protect, but Satan sought to regain an earthly form of the authority and power he literally threw away when he rebelled against God. And he regained that power at our expense.

One of the concepts we'll introduce in chapter seven, dealing with what we call "counter-covenant," details Satan's tireless efforts to deceive us by counterfeiting every good thing that God produces, including relationships. We are now ready for formal definitions of satanic-type beings. This information also harkens back to chapter one and the discussion we referred to earlier, about the differences between devils and demons, which eventually brought this book project together in the first place.

1) A *devil* is a fallen angel (a cherub, a seraph, or a teraph), which is often referred to in scripture as an "evil spirit." As far as we know, all fallen angels were part of the original (and only) anti-God, anti-heaven rebellion, led by Lucifer/Satan. In Hebrew, fallen teraphim ("watchers") are also known as *sayir*. The ancient Greeks and Babylonians called them *satyrs*.

2) A *nephal* (plural: *nephilim*) is the offspring from the mating of a teraph with a woman, as detailed previously in Genesis 6:1–2. However, in Genesis 6:4, note that the "divine beings" and "sons of God" of various translations are clearly identified as nephilim in Genesis 6:4:

> The Nephilim were on the earth in those days, and also afterward, when the sons of God came in to the daughters of men, and they bore children to them. Those were the mighty men who were of old, men of renown.

As we mentioned above, the literal meaning of the word nephal is "a living abortion" or "to fall to the ground." Both the pre-Flood and post-Flood giants of Numbers 13:33, Deuteronomy 3:11, and II Samuel 21:22 were nephilim (although it's important to recognize that not *all* post-Flood nephilim grow to unusual size).

Many of the "people" living in Canaan before the Israelites conquered the land were actually nephilim (remember, as shown above, in Genesis 6:4, they definitely *did* reappear on the earth after the flood), which helps explain why God commanded the Israelites to obliterate them utterly, as in the flood. Another famous nephal, of course, was Goliath, whom David defeated with a stone between the eyeballs. Nephilim are also referred to as "men of renown" or "men of old" (Genesis 6:4, Numbers 16:2).

3) A *demon* is the disembodied soul of a dead nephal. Demons are often referred to in Scripture as "unclean spirits."

Of these three, devils are by far the most powerful. That's why Yeshua made such a clear distinction between devils and demons. By contrast, the demons residing within the Gadarene madman, as detailed in the fifth chapter of Mark and the eighth chapter of Luke, came out readily even though their numbers were "legion." Note also that they begged Yeshua not to send them "into the void" but into living things, even though the nearby herd of pigs was their only real choice. Demons always seek to reside inside something living; they'll readily choose animals if no humans are available. Even pigs!

So what are demons?

According to Enoch's ancient account, the fallen angels (devils) that produced the nephilim also taught man forbidden things, such as sorcery, the perverted use of medicinal herbs, sexual deviance, and violent warfare. The nephilim had a penchant for bloodshed, as detailed in Genesis 6:11–13:

> Now the earth was corrupt in the sight of God, and
> the earth was filled with violence. God looked on
> the earth, and behold, it was corrupt; for all flesh
> had corrupted their way upon the earth. Then God
> said to Noah, "The end of all flesh has come before
> Me; for the earth is filled with violence because of
> them; and behold, I am about to destroy them with
> the earth."

What we're telling you now might not seem completely clear in our English versions of Genesis. The Hebrew text, along with the book of Enoch, fills in the crucial details. *Despite the popular interpretation to the effect that God killed millions of people by bringing on the Flood, He was actually destroying nephilim and those in league with them.*

Noah and his family were the only human beings left on the earth who were not either tainted by nephilim blood or in league with the nephilim. By bringing Noah and his uncorrupted family through alone, God was *saving* man from total corruption, from total extinction in the God-breathed, Holy Spirit-infused form He Himself had originally created.

So, Noah built an ark and gathered his family and all those animals on board. The Flood cleansed the earth of the genetic impurities introduced through the union of devils and the daughters of man. The offspring of the original nephilim were killed and Satan was checkmated, just as God had promised.

Now, all the nephilim who were living at that time were destroyed by the Flood, thus re-purifying the human race by limiting it to the the blood descendants of Noah. But unfortunately, though the bodies of the nephilim were obliterated, their half-devil, half-human souls "lived" on, wandering the earth, seeking habitation. That was the unavoidable consequence of all that intentional sin and perversion.

The ancient Hebrews called these souls "unclean spirits" or "demons." Thus, *demons are the disembodied souls of nephilim.* And, of course, the receding of the Flood waters did not signal a total end to the physical nephilim, either. The Bible is very clear in explaining that the nephilim reestablished themselves after the flood, by reemerging in the same way as before. Once again, here's what Genesis 6:4 says (emphasis added):

> The Nephilim were on the earth in those days, *and also afterward*, when the sons of God came in to the daughters of men, and they bore children to them. Those were the mighty men who were of old, men of renown.

How do we know where demons come from?

Two separate Hebrew words are used to refer to demons – *tamunefal* and *nefsheraa*. The first half of the word tamunefal (*tamu*) means "one who is buried or dead." Obviously, a fallen angel (which would be a devil) can't be buried.

The second half of the word *tamunefal* (*nefal*) is the singular for nephilim, which (as we have just established) are the offspring of sexual unions between fallen angels and women. So, the word tamunefal literally means "a dead nephal." Some additional meanings are "a hidden abortion, polluted, defiled, an unclean spirit."

The second word for demons, *nefsheraa*, is also compound – *nefesh* (animal soul) and *raa* (evil). The word *nefesh*, as we've explained elsewhere in this chapter, denotes an animal soul, which all life possesses. So *nefsheraa* literally means an "evil animal soul" or "the soul of an evil beast." It can also be translated as "a disembodied soul, deformed, wicked, a hungry soul, an evil soul."

Unfortunately, the Hebrew words for devil are still sometimes interpreted in our English translations as "demon," by translators who simply do not know the difference. English versions interchange and do not differentiate. And that is why we still see so much confusion.

Don't feel sorry for the nephilim

Before we leave this subject entirely, we think it's also important to point out one of those self-evident truths – something that will be entirely obvious once we say it, but which might not come into clear focus if we don't. The nature of God is to protect what He values; to shield His own creation from harm. And as servants, friends, inheritors, and eventually the bride of Yeshua, we must always be grateful for such protection.

At the same time, God takes no pleasure in destroying anything. And yet, as the ultimate source of righteousness, He simply cannot do otherwise with various "powers and principalities" that have arisen to work directly against His holy creation. Please bear that in mind when you consider what the Lord did, via the flood, to the nephilim of old. Or, when you remember what He would have done to the nephilim in the land of Canann, had the children of Israel been fully obedient and destroyed those He commanded them to destroy.

The nephilim do not deserve our misplaced pity. Indeed, given their nature and their source, they have no capacity whatsoever to become redeemed of God. As Jude 1:19 put it:

> It is these who are [agitators] setting up distinctions and causing divisions – merely sensual [creatures, carnal, worldly minded people], devoid of the [Holy] Spirit and destitute of any higher spiritual life. (AMP)

In other words, the nephilim are lower than the animals. Worse yet, they are many times more dangerous, wicked, and capable of harming us than any wild beast we might ever encounter. Isaiah calls them "detestable ones" (Isaiah 24:16). In addition, they are completely empty of any spiritual or emotional resemblance to human beings. All humanity has the spark of God dwelling within it; literally, we are God-breathed. Thus it's a complete contradiction of terms if we try to apply "human" attributes to nephilim.

Nephilim are not necessarily extinct . . .

We would like to report that "living" nephilim are entirely creatures of the distant past – that maybe a few new ones were born after the Flood, but that the Israelites wiped them all out when they conquered Canaan and they've never been reproduced since then. But of course we can't certify any such thing. Consider just a few clues . . .

◆ When various speakers in the B'rit Hadashah talked about "false prophets" they used various idiomatic Hebraic terms that referred directly back to earlier terms for the nephilim – for example, "men of old" and "men of renown." Obviously, nephilim were still around in those days. Consider what the Lord tells us in II Peter 2:12–19:

> [12] But these, like unreasoning animals, born as creatures of instinct to be captured and killed, reviling where they have no knowledge, will in the destruction of those creatures also be destroyed, [13] suffering wrong as the wages of doing wrong. They count it a pleasure to revel in the daytime. They are stains and blemishes, reveling in their deceptions, as they carouse with you, [14] having eyes full of adultery that never cease from sin, enticing unstable souls, having a heart trained in greed, accursed children; [15] forsaking the right way, they have gone astray, having followed the way of Balaam, the son of Beor, who loved the wages of unrighteousness; [16] but he received a rebuke for his own transgression, for a mute donkey, speaking with a voice of a man, restrained the madness of the prophet. [17] These are springs without water and mists driven

by a storm, for whom the black darkness has been reserved. [18] For speaking out arrogant words of vanity they entice by fleshly desires, by sensuality, those who barely escape from the ones who live in error, [19] promising them freedom while they themselves are slaves of corruption; for by what a man is overcome, by this he is enslaved.

The NIV translation of the Bible renders the last three verses of the above (17–19) as follows:

These men are springs without water and mists driven by a storm. *Blackest darkness is reserved for them.* For they mouth empty, boastful words and, by appealing to the lust-ful desires of sinful human nature, they entice people who are just escaping from those who live in error. They promise them freedom, while they themselves are slaves of depravity – for a man is a slave to what-ever has mastered him. (Italics added)

We would also encourage you to re-read the book of Jude, which essentially contains all the same warnings.

In talking about the outward signs of his return, Yeshua said, in Luke 17:26–27:

"And [just] as it was in the days of Noah, so will it be in the time of the Son of Man. [People] ate, *they* drank, *they* married, *they* were given in marriage, right up to the day when Noah went into the ark, and the flood came and destroyed them all" (AMP – Ital-ics added).

What's unique about that passage?

When has there ever been a time when people didn't eat, drink or marry? How can activities which have gone on since the creation, be a sign that will tip us off to the return of Yeshua?

Well, the words from which translaters got "they" were the Hebrew words *baal* (*devils*) *nashim* (*women*), which mean "devils/idols" and "women." In other words, this passage is saying that, "as it was in the days of Noah when '*devils and women*' were given in marriage, etc., etc."

This makes far more contextual sense. Yeshua is saying that one sign of the end times will be the clear spectacle of fallen angels, giving and taking in marriage and once more producing nephilim. And in effect, God is saying that He is simply not going to put up with such abominations. He didn't put up with it in ancient times and He's not going to put up with it in the end times, either. On the contrary, He's coming back to end it once and for all.

This is further supported by Daniel 2:43–44:

And as you saw the iron mixed with miry and earthen clay, so they shall mingle themselves in the seed of men [in marriage bonds]; but they will not hold together [for two such elements or ideologies can never harmonize], even as iron does not mingle itself with clay. And in the days of these [final ten] kings shall the God of heaven set up a kingdom which shall never be destroyed, nor shall its sovereignty be left to another people; but it shall break and crush and consume all these kingdoms and it shall stand forever. (AMP)

Here, Daniel talks about the statue he sees in his vision, and refers to the four evil kingdoms, represented by gold, silver, bronze, and the feet that were made of iron mixed with clay.

This statue is a representation of the last four kingdoms that will rule Earth, starting with Nebuchadnezzar. Others have already interpreted much of this passage correctly; the first three metals refer to Babylon, Medo-Persia, and Greece. The feet represent the final kingdom that will be governed by the Beast we refer to as the antichrist.

But Daniel is saying something else, too – something often missed. According to Hebraic symbology, clay is the sign for man. Indeed, the word "Adamah" (whence comes the name "Adam"; thus, within the first man's name is a direct reference to where he came from) literally means "soil," and iron is the sign for angels operating on the earth. Therefore, within the Kingdom of the Beast, Daniel is prophesying that there will once again be a commingling between man and devils.

In other words, just as Yeshua said in Luke 17:26–27, this familiar passage from Daniel, written long before Yeshua came the first time, is prophesying that teraphim will be having intercourse and producing offspring *as they did in the days of Noah*, just before Yeshua comes back for the final time.

Now . . . does all of this mean that we'll be seeing nephilim in the end times? Yes, it does! But does it mean we'll be seeing giants? Not necessarily. Remember what we said earlier – the nephilim we're likely to see will be much more normal in appearance than the giants of the pre- and immediate post-Flood eras. The nephilim most likely to be present at the end times will be a type that doesn't take on giant proportions.

What is the nephilim agenda?

If devils are scripturally defined as "fallen angels," (although they can, as we've shown, take on human appearance), and demons are the souls of the physical offspring (nephilim) of devils and humans, then what can we know or infer about each of their separate agendas? For example, how should our understanding affect the way we deal with them when we are casting out or discerning spirits (I Corinthians 12:10)?

First, we know that the disembodied nephilim are striving for their lost humanity. For example, recall the Gadarene madman. Whenever a manifestation such as that occurs, as described in Matthew 5, we're talking about a demonic presence. Nephilim feed on the sensations of humans. Demons want to feel our fear, our hate, our pain, our lust, or any other human emotion.

So, they control their host to create intense sensation – painful or pleasurable, it doesn't matter. Demons just want to feed on the sensory stimulation – to feel "human" again. These foul creatures are the fragmented remains of something that was once partially human. All true humanity has authority over them, but *in the name of Yeshua only*. They use fear and intimidation to try to convince us otherwise, but we need not be fooled.

What about devils?

Whereas demons want to feed on human experience regardless of the cost to the host involved, we believe that devils want more. It follows logically that devils want your identity and the authority that God gave uniquely to each one of us. They are by nature territorial, refusing to share their possessions with any other devils. They don't mind sharing a person with a host of demons, however. Demons don't interfere with the identity devils crave.

When you exercise authority and eliminate demonic influence, you may very well attract the attention of more dangerous beings. The presence of a devil is indicated when your purpose, identity, vision, and authority come under assault. Even Yeshua experienced this type of encounter as Satan began his attack with the words: "*If you are the Son of God*" (Matthew 4:3).

Be careful, not arrogant, in confronting any supernatural entity lest you fall when you think you stand. Dealing with devils requires a lifestyle of prayer and fasting to establish authority in submission to the Almighty (Matthew 17:14–21). Even the archangel Michael didn't rebuke Satan directly; as referenced in Jude 9, he petitioned God to deal with him: "The *Lord* rebuke you."

The battles in the Garden and at the Flood were won by God. The strategies of Satan were deterred and God's plan for man was continued. We are both the *inheritors* and the *instruments* of that plan, as long as we maintain close relationships with God, through the covenants, and do as He instructs.

In summary . . .

- Devils are fallen angels – teraphim, seraphim, or cherubim.
- Teraphim, the lowest order of angels, can take human form and interbreed with women.
- The offspring of a teraphim and a woman is called a nephal (plural: nephilim).
- Demons were not created by God; they are the disembodied souls of dead nephilim.
- Therefore, *devils and demons are not the same thing!* And in their present forms, neither one was created by God. They both result from a rebellion among the heavenly host that God never intended. They each have separate agendas. And, when we encounter them we must deal with them differently.
- Most important of all, devils and demons have not gone away. They are not just part of the ancient past; they are with us now and will be with us in horrid abundance during the end times. In the second volume in this series we will deal with this subject again; for now, forewarned is forearmed.

5

Menorah

Imagine a teacher with a roomful of first-graders spread out in front of her, each one with twelve little red blocks on his desk. First she asks them to push the whole pile over to one side, then to "take three away" to the other side, then to count what's left.

She has just given those kids a graphic demonstration of how subtraction works in the real world. In the process, rather than exercising their brains only, the students have engaged (1) their intellects, (2) their sense of sight, and (3) their sense of touch. And, if they had used chocolate candies instead of wooden blocks they also would have engaged their senses of (4) smell and (5) taste! Better still, if they'd been asked to verbalize what they were doing, *as they did it,* they would have used oral language, too, which is one of the best reinforcers of all.

Why does any of this matter? Because, the more we engage our "separate faculties" in the learning process, the more quickly we learn and the longer we retain new material.

This kind of thing is nothing new. Instructors in all kinds of classrooms have used what is now called "multisensory teaching" for generations. The goal is to create a lasting impression – something memorable – that conveys a clear message. If that "lasting impression" is a mental image, fine. If the mental image is also linked to a physical action, even better. If that "multi-dimensioned" image is further connected to a sound and a smell, that's even better . . . and so on.

However, despite how frequently and creatively such methods have been employed over the centuries, in thousands and thousands of situations in which people have developed efficient methods for *learning and retaining information*, the methods themselves were never entirely original to man.[1] To consider just one illustration from the Bible, recall what happened in the book of Ezekiel, in chapters 40 through 43, when the Lord gave Ezekiel a clear vision of the Third (Millennial) Temple.

First, God introduced Ezekiel to a man who was "like bronze," clearly a memorable mental image. *Second*, Ezekiel noted that the man had a linen cord and a measuring rod in his hand, two important details leading to the next step, both of which Ezekiel could see and almost feel. *Third*, the man took Ezekiel on a tour of the temple, during which Ezekiel *watched him take each measurement, probably repeated each one out loud, noted the exact measurement in his written record (either right away or soon thereafter), and thereby imprinted the information clearly on his brain.*

Without knowing it, Ezekiel was using one of the most effective "comprehension" techniques ever developed, called *Visualization/ Verbalization*.[2] In other words, God has always been way ahead of the game! Because He designed the human brain Himself, He has always been into "learning reinforcement" of all kinds. We sometimes call this "symbolism." However, when God is in charge, this kind of teaching often serves a much larger purpose than just connecting a simple concept with a single symbol.

A huge metaphor

As we have already shown, the first five books of the Bible mirror the ancient Hebrew ketubah, or marriage contract. Once you know something about the Hebrew roots of Scripture, the symbolism seems impossible to miss. Through the betrothal covenant, God intends to remarry His people, who divorced Him in the Garden of

Eden. He put the marriage contract in force thousands of years ago. He simply had to provide a way to fulfill the covenant, which is where His Son came into the picture.

Meanwhile, to further the above metaphor, as events slowly build to the coming of Yeshua, God speaks over and over again of the pure relationship between bride and groom. Of harmonious interactions between husband and wife. Of the details of the marriage ritual, of bearing children and bequeathing an honorable inheritance, of eternal rewards that build up naturally as a result.

And yet, as central as the betrothal/marriage covenant is to the message God has for us, it's not the only sustained metaphor He uses. There's another one, tied to a sacred object that God Himself designed, which resonates almost as powerfully throughout the scriptures.

We're talking about the *menorah* metaphor, which really comes into its own in the book of Revelation. There it becomes a literal framework on which the chapters and verses of John's apocalyptic vision can be hung, like branches and leaves on a tree.

At the same time, the betrothal and menorah metaphors complement each other perfectly. They illuminate each other; each one expands the meaning of the other. Yet they are slightly different, for the *betrothal/marriage* metaphor is largely about *concepts* while the *menorah* metaphor is largely about *structure*.

Put another way, the marriage metaphor tells us *how God thinks about us*. The menorah metaphor shows us His plan for restoring His bride to Himself. It also shows us *how He organized* the book of Revelation, and much of the prophetic and historical information contained in the Tanakh, to lead us forward into His truth. And much of that truth, so much easier to identify and assimilate by way of the menorah metaphor, begins to emerge in succeeding chapters, even before we begin the next volume. That's why we're introducing the concept here, even though it won't really come into its own as our *foundational,* or *structural,* metaphor until we get to Revelation itself.

Now, can we explain and substantiate all this? Well, certainly not without starting at the beginning. So let's get a little more background . . .

Symbolism in the Israelite camp

Even when they set up their tents for a single night, the children of Israel laid out their camp in a pattern that was clearly established by the Lord. As with everything else that comes from His hand, in His great wisdom the Lord provided all of us, as well, with a clear, metaphorical picture of how He wants us to approach Him. Many people believe we can approach God in any way we want, but over and over again He has given us clearly delineated details on how He wants us to develop an intimate relationship with Him.

Basically, the Lord divided the Israelite camp into four main sections. As we will demonstrate momentarily, each section then corresponded to one of the covenants (servanthood, friendship, inheritance, and marriage) that make up the fabric of God's desired relationship with us.

Each section of the camp modeled a particular aspect of God's invitation to each of us. The Lord never tires of inviting us to increase our intimacy and draw closer to Him through enhanced covenant. Thus the defining element for each section of the camp was proximity to the Lord Himself, who was located at the very center. He put His tabernacle in the middle and put Himself in a definite spot inside, in the Holy of Holies, symbolizing His desired place within our lives.

Again, in technical terms it's called . . . *the center!* Everything in our lives should revolve around Him. All other sections within the camp modeled a definite "linkage" to God, but the closer you got to the Holy of Holies the closer you got to a face-to-face relationship.

It's also worth noting that, symbolically, every dividing line of every section of the camp, whether a wall, a curtain, or the beginning of the wilderness, represented separation from God – or, reduced intimacy. But it also symbolized increasing protection for those who were inside more and more boundaries. It showed how God covets His bride. Where does He put her? Of course – right in the center, with minimum vulnerability to outside forces. In like measure, increased covenant relationship enhances our ability to stand against the escalating deceptions of Satan.

Outside the camp = death

Conversely, in metaphorical terms, the area outside the camp equaled death. This is where all the refuse went, where all the trash was buried, where anything sick or defiled was kept. It was also where women went during their monthly cycles, not as punishment but to separate them physically from the others (and perhaps to remove temptation from their husbands). They were ushered into a protected area, were sheltered in comfortable tents, and were well-guarded and well-cared for.

For ancient Hebrew women, blood equaled life and a loss of blood equaled a loss of life. So this was a time of mourning; in essence they were sitting shiva[3] for the life that had not come to be. In ancient Hebrew thought, such a woman, through natural events, had come in contact with the dead. According to God's own laws, that meant she could not come in sexual contact with her husband until a certain purification period had passed.

How did the four sections relate to the four covenants?[4]

For now, as briefly as possible, let us examine each of the four sections of the camp as they relate to covenant, so we can then talk knowledgeably about the menorah.

1) *The main camp itself, which equaled servanthood*
   If you could have flown over the Israelite's camp, perhaps on the back of an eagle, you would have seen a vast assemblage of people, numbering three million or more and extending over a broad area of up to ten square miles.

   All the people lived in the vast outer area of the camp proper. That's where they lived their daily lives–where they kept their flocks, pitched their tents, made their clothes, did their cooking, and disciplined their children. It was also where they learned to serve their God, humbly, by fulfilling

His principles for daily living (the *mishpatim*). In the words of Paul, this is where the people "died daily" to themselves. This part of the camp mirrors the blood (service) covenant.

In the same way, even today, as we enter into God's salvation, in metaphorical terms we step into God's camp – His protection, His covering, and a certain level of relationship with Him. There's more to be had as we move toward the center, but here at the outer edge the young believer begins his walk and establishes his developing relationship, through covenant, with the Lord. God expects us to begin with servanthood, the first covenant that He calls us into. He lays out His principles for our lives in Torah and B'rit Hadashah, and He expects us to begin dying daily to our own evil desires. At the same time He expects us to honor His principles, thereby fulfilling the responsibilities of servanthood.

2) *The Outer Court, which equaled friendship*
As you flew on the eagle's back toward the middle of the camp, you would immediately recognize the portable tabernacle standing at the very center. From the air it surely would have looked majestic, its clean, straight, "regular" lines clearly setting it apart from the surrounding diorama.

Not all of this would be obvious from the air, but it was made up of three distinctly different sections – an outer court, an inner court, and the oft-cited "Holy of Holies" inside the inner court.

The outer court measured approximately 150 by 75 feet (100 x 50 cubits) and was bounded by a metal framework that supported walls of heavy curtains (but no roof). Near the eastern end of the outer court you would see the only entrance, and a large bronze altar just inside, to which the people of the camp brought sacrifices to be offered up to God on their behalf by the priests. The outer court also contained a large bronze laver in which the priests could wash (cleanse) themselves.

The tabernacle stood at the very center of the camp. As large as it might have seemed, its outer court was tiny compared to the vast camp. Everyone was allowed in to make reparations for their sins, but obviously not all at once.

Entering the tabernacle brought you one major step closer to the presence of God. The people who worked here were entrusted with greater levels of responsibility. They also walked in greater authority (i.e., the right to act in the capacity of someone else), just as a friend, in an ancient community or household, might have walked (or acted) on behalf of another. In stark contrast to a master/servant relationship, this one mirrored the salt (friendship) covenant. At the same time, recall that those acting on behalf of others (i.e., friendship covenant) also lived their daily lives in the outer camp, so they were also walking in service to God.

3) *The inner court of the tabernacle, which equaled sonship*
Next, as you flew even closer to the exact center of the camp you would see the tabernacle proper. From the air it might look somewhat like a long, lovingly crafted, flat-topped bunkhouse, 45 by 15 feet (30 x 10 cubits), which made it symmetrical to the larger outer court as a whole. Located at the western end of the outer court, it was surrounded on three sides by solid walls made of interconnected planks of acacia wood, set by tenons (i.e., "tabs," or extensions of the wood) into brass sockets that rested on the ground. Its eastern end opened onto the outer court, but was walled off to all but the priests by a large curtain that hung from six pillars.

In contrast to the outer court, the tabernacle had a roof. The sidewalls were draped with four layers of heavy materials,[5] which extended from one wall to the opposite side, formed a roof, and thus made the whole thing look somewhat like a "tent within a tent."

Internally, though you couldn't see this from the air, the tabernacle was divided into two separate rooms by a heavy, double curtain of the finest workmanship. The curtain was put in place both to safeguard us and to remind us of the twofold nature of God's protection, which sheltered us from both outside harm and from the kind of "internal" harm (i.e., dying!) that could come about from approaching, in a state of sin, too close to the Holy God.

As you passed through the curtain, from the outer court, you would enter the inner court, measuring 30 by 15 feet (20 x 10 cubits). Here you would encounter three pieces of furniture, (1) a golden altar of incense, (2) a golden table that held twelve loaves of show bread (changed every week), and (3) a golden, seven-stemmed menorah that stood about six feet tall and provided the only light for the inner court.

The significance of the inner court lay in the degree of intimacy it offered to the chosen priests. Only select ones were ever allowed to enter. This holy place mirrored the sandal (inheritance) covenant. Remember when Moses was told to take off his sandals because he was standing on holy ground? The priests who entered the inner court were like sons of God, entering a holy place in their bare feet.

In terms of the Israelites' overall association with God, this room was the second most intimate location in the camp. As with the covenants, each of which serves as the foundation for the next, greater responsibility was both *conferred on* and *required of* all who entered the inner court. In the same way, as we grow into maturity with Him, God gives us greater and greater levels of both authority and responsibility, just as Yeshua explained in the parable of the talents (Matthew 25:14–30). Thus all good fathers plan for their sons and daughters to inherit what they themselves have owned, and prepare them accordingly.

4) *The Holy of Holies, which equaled marriage*
The inner court in the tabernacle was separated from the next room by another elaborate veil, doubling once again as both a curtain for the priests' protection and an entryway into greater intimacy and responsibility. The room beyond the veil was known as the "holy place," "the holiest," the "sanctuary," and the "first tabernacle." It was a cube, 15 by 15 feet (10 x 10 cubits).

However, most people know this room as the *Holy of Holies*. The Holy of Holies was not illuminated in any way by any manmade device. But it was not kept in complete darkness, for God Himself literally made His home here among the Israelites. His glory provided whatever illumination He desired.

The Holy of Holies contained just one piece of furniture, the Ark of the Covenant,[6] displaying the two golden cherubim between whose outspread wings sat the mercy seat of God. If God were in the mercy seat, facing the altar, the menorah on the other side of the veil would be on his right. Therefore the menorah stood, literally, at the right hand of God.

Only the High Priest, carefully chosen for both the "terror and the honor,"[7] was ever allowed to enter, and then only once a year on the great Day of Atonement (*Yom Kippur*). He wore a bell and attached himself to a strong rope. If the bell ever stopped ringing, for any length of time, the priests on the other side could assume that he'd not been found sufficiently holy for the honor of approaching God directly, and therefore had died. They could then use the rope to pull him back out.

The Holy of Holies represented total intimacy via the ultimate covenant with God Himself, betrothal/marriage. But until Yeshua died on the cross, God had a very strict set of rules detailing who could approach Him, and how. Even those who had entered into the more intimate covenants, by coming into the inner court, were still separated by a heavy veil to protect them from His presence. But when Yeshua died that final veil was ripped, both literally and figuratively, from top to bottom.

Approaching a holy God

Symbolically, the ripping of the veil made two rooms into one, revealing how God sees marriage. Do not two become one? Those who have entered into the highest covenant as His inheritors, those who have been given his authority and protection, are suddenly no longer separated from Him. Indeed, in Hebrews 4:16, doesn't B'rit Hadashah tell us that now we have the right to come before the throne boldly?

Actually, this is a classical misinterpretation. In Hebraic understanding, to "come before the throne" meant to stop at the curtain. The curtain was rent but it was still at the edge of the Holy of Holies, and still delineated the limits of our access. Our intermediary now is our High Priest, Yeshua, who has paid the ultimate price (Heb. 5:10). And He proceeds to the Holy Seat and has a face-to-face relationship with God the Father. We see him face-to-face, but we are not IN his face.

We can come to the edge and look in toward the Holy of Holies, but only one person at a time is ever permitted to enter. And Scripture tells us, in several places, that that "one person" is now Yeshua, our High Priest. He now acts as the only intermediary between God and man, as explained in the last three verses of chapter seven and the first two verses of chapter eight of Hebrews:

> For it was fitting for us to have such a high priest, holy, innocent, undefiled, separated from sinners and exalted above the heavens; who does not need daily, like those high priests, to offer up sacrifices, first for His own sins and then for the sins of the people, because this He did once for all when He offered up Himself. For the Law appoints men as

high priests who are weak, but the word of the oath, which came after the Law, appoints a Son, made perfect forever. (Hebrews 7:26-28)

Now the main point in what has been said is this: we have such a high priest, who has taken His seat at the right hand of the throne of the Majesty in the heavens, a minister in the sanctuary and in the true tabernacle, which the Lord pitched, not man. (Hebrews 8:1-2)

If every believer could enter the Holy of Holies anytime he wanted to, that would nullify the need for a High Priest. But that's not how it works – given the way God set up the system, if you took away the priesthood you would literally take away salvation. As the above passage from Hebrews explains, Yeshua is our High Priest, acting as the one who brings the cleansing, which is Himself, so that God can see us as righteous, without sin, and worthy of His presence.

The menorah as a sacred symbol

Even as the shekinah glory of God gave the only light within the sacred Holy of Holies, the menorah gave the only light within the inner court. But where did the menorah come from?

In the book of Exodus, starting with chapter 25, the Lord gave Moses very clear instructions on how to make the tabernacle and all its contents. He told Moses how to make the Ark of the Covenant, the table, the altar of burnt offerings, the priestly garments, numerous sacred implements, and various other pieces of equipment. All these things were to be used in worshipping Him and in transporting and protecting the tabernacle and its furnishings.

The Lord also anointed and enabled certain craftsmen to serve Him, as in Exodus 35: 30–33:

... the LORD has called by name Bezalel the son of Uri, the son of Hur, of the tribe of Judah. "And He has filled him with the Spirit of God, in wisdom, in understanding and in knowledge and in all crafts-manship; to make designs for working in gold and in silver and in bronze, and in the cutting of stones for settings and in the carving of wood, so as to per-form in every inventive work.

In plain language, the Lord poured supernatural skill into Bezalel, sufficient for the job God had in mind. For example, mak-ing the original menorah required hand-hammering into shape a single lump of pure gold weighing just over ninety pounds.[8]

The golden menorah had seven branches, arranged in linear fashion, one in the center and three on either side. All seven branches were hollow, so the oil could flow along wicks tapping into three reservoirs built into the central branch, or trunk. The oil itself came from the "weeping" of olives that were beaten until bruised, but not pressed. The oil represented the *Holy Spirit* and was the purest fuel available for the seven flames, which provided the only illumination for the inner court. The symbolism is hard to miss – the light of God should be the only source of light leading us through life.

Because the flames represented the holy presence of God Him-self, He required them to be kept lit at all times. Every morning, the priests replaced the bowls at the top of each of the seven branches with clean bowls filled with a reservoir of fresh oil, and trimmed each of the wicks. As you might expect, the discarded trimmings were buried outside the camp.

Why such an extreme step? Well, a blackened wick cannot sup-port a clean, pure flame. As with sin, uncleanness disrupts. The flame staggers and sputters and gives off less light. In the same way, sin blackens our lives and requires trimming, circumcision, and even-tual banishment outside the boundaries of our own encampments.

The six branches represent mankind

The branches of ancient menorahs were designed with a leaf pattern and were recognized as depicting the Tree of Life. The form of the menorah derives from the shape of a burning or lighted tree. The burning bush upon which the Spirit of the Lord rested in Exodus 3:2–4 was a foreshadowing of the menorah.

The center lamp was referred to as the *ner tamid* or "eternal light" (Leviticus 24:2). This particular light is also called the *shamash*, or "servant," because it was used to rekindle the remaining six lights on the menorah whenever they were trimmed. The Hebrew word for "sun" is also *shamash*, and the sun is considered the servant-light to the natural world. The sun was created on the fourth day just as the shamash holds the fourth position on a menorah.

Ancient Hebrew rabbis have suggested that this shamash position represents Messiah. The shamash is also called the plumb line (Zechariah 4:1–14). A plumb line is used in construction as the true level for establishing the foundation of a new building, just as Messiah's life should be the true and correct foundation for our lives. Yeshua is the source of strength and light from which we glorify the Father.

The six branches coming from the sides of the shamash represent mankind, even as we were created on the sixth day. When connected to the main branch they find their source of fuel to produce light. He is the vine; we are the branches (John 15:1–8). Yeshua as the shamash is the centerpiece of the human race. Isaiah 11:1 prophesied the first coming of Yeshua, describing Him as a shoot that would spring from the stem of Jesse, a branch that would grow out of his roots. The Hebrew word for "branch" is *netzer*, from which the town of Nazareth derives its name. It is a seemingly insignificant little branch, ("Can anything good come out of Nazareth?" [John 1:46]), yet this branch, Yeshua, became the shamash of the Tree of Life, the Vine through which life flows to the branches.

Like the menorah in which oil flows from the shamash, Yeshua provides the oil of the Holy Spirit to us. We, in turn, have been commissioned by Him to be the lights of the world (Matthew 5:14). In Isaiah 11:2 we see Yeshua as the Branch that the Spirit of the Lord rests upon and ignites with six other spirits: wisdom, understanding, counsel, power, knowledge, and fear of the Lord. The presence of God is the holy fire that ignites His people, so that we, like the living branches of a golden menorah, shine forth and bring light to a darkened world.

At the same time, as God's people, we are not the *source* of the light and we are not the *fuel*. As the menorah branches are hollow, we should be willing conduits for God's holiness and His light, leading into the knowledge and understanding of how to serve Him. We are the conduits for His message to the rest of the world. If we allow the Spirit of God to flow through us we thereby accomplish God's will, which is to spread the good news throughout the world. Matthew 5:14–16 expresses this concept perfectly:

> "You are the light of the world. A city set on a hill cannot be hidden; nor does anyone light a lamp and put it under a basket, but on the lampstand, and it gives light to all who are in the house. Let your light shine before men in such a way that they may see your good works, and glorify your Father who is in heaven."

The menorah as Revelation's master pattern

Okay. We've talked about the menorah quite a bit but we still haven't explained why we call it the "foundational metaphor" for the book of Revelation! Let's do that now.

In the first chapter of Ezekiel, in his first recorded vision, the prophet encountered something extraordinary. He described what he saw as a brilliant light encircled by a rainbow of colored fire and concentric "wheels within wheels." Centuries later, as recorded in Revelation, the apostle John saw something equally baffling – seven shining golden lampstands with someone standing in their midst, glowing as brightly as molten metal.

Between these two accounts we read of shining rainbows, sapphire seas, winged creatures circling and shouting, thunders roaring, and lightning flashing. And in the center of all this frenzied activity, God stands alone like the nucleus of an atom, while everything glows and spins and whirls around Him.

What are Ezekiel and John trying to convey? Like the blind men feeling an elephant in the familiar story, could both of these men be describing the very same thing, but from their own unique perspectives?

Our research indicates that the throne of God described in Ezekiel 1:15–28, and the seven lampstands of Revelation 1:12–20, are one and the same. The seven branches on the lampstand seen by John all had a unique feature. Each separate branch was also an entire seven-branched menorah unto itself, like the "wheels within wheels" described by Ezekiel. As flames crown the wheels and angels fly in and out, we get the impression of a spinning menorah.

Ezekiel also says that this object is God's throne, which corresponds to the throne/menorah description in Revelation 4:1–6:

> After these things I looked, and behold, a door standing open in heaven, and the first voice which I had heard, like the sound of a trumpet speaking with me, said, "Come up here, and I will show you what must take place after these things."
> [2] Immediately I was in the Spirit; and behold, a throne was standing in heaven, and One sitting on the throne. [3] And He who was sitting was like a jasper stone and a sardius in appearance; and there was a rainbow around the throne, like an emerald in appearance. [4] Around the throne were twenty-four thrones; and upon the thrones I saw twenty-four elders sitting, clothed in white garments, and golden crowns on their heads.

[5] Out from the throne come flashes of lightning and sounds and peals of thunder. And there were seven lamps of fire burning before the throne, which are the seven Spirits of God; [6] and before the throne there was something like a sea of glass, like crystal; and in the center and around the throne, four living creatures full of eyes in front and behind.

Even before the above, in Revelation 2 and 3, John is instructed to write letters to seven churches in Asia Minor. These are also represented as seven golden menorahs. Again, the foundation for understanding Revelation can be found right here, among all this evidence taken from vastly separated portions of the Bible yet interwoven together, in the Lord's own inimitable "multisensory" style, into a multi-reinforced, unmistakable image.

This configuration is the master pattern for the entire book of Revelation. The seven menorahs become a massive superstructure for organizing all the details that follow, all the way through to the end of the Bible.

However, to appreciate what we're saying you first have to sort, arrange, coordinate, and then *study* the events of Revelation. You do this, first, by positioning them on the master menorah, then by examining them from that perspective, carefully considering them in context *as they relate to each other.* At that point, the individual events begin to fit together, *within the overall scenario.* And then they "suddenly" make far more sense than from any other viewpoint.

Through the seven interlinked menorahs we are introduced to forty-nine events, arranged in seven groups of seven. We refer to them as the . . .

- ◆ Seven Letters
- ◆ Seven Seals
- ◆ Seven Trumpets
- ◆ Seven Thunders
- ◆ Seven Bowls

- ◆ Seven Angelic Proclamations
- ◆ Seven Evil Kingdoms

To put each of these in its proper place, you have to realize that some go on the right side (the Lord's covenant side), and some are assigned to the left side (Satan's counter-covenant side – more about this in chapter 7). Then, just as the lamps on the original menorah were always lit from right to left, so events on the menorah occur in right to left order.

It sounds complicated, but once you get the basic organization figured out you realize how precisely everything fits together. It seems exactly like a masterplan God would develop, complex enough so that it isn't immediately obvious to everyone, yet fundamentally simple. Detailed enough to challenge the most painstaking researcher, yet symmetrical and logical in every tiny detail.

Again, the words we quoted from Proverbs way back at the beginning of chapter one of this book come to mind: "It is the glory of God to conceal a matter, but the glory of kings is to search out a matter" (Proverbs 25:2).

Revelation thus becomes a clear, logical chronology, a blow-by-blow account of the awesome events that will usher in the second coming of Yeshua. But that doesn't mean we're ready to unravel it yet! We still have several chapters and several more fundamental concepts to put in place before we tackle the mysteries of the book of Revelation in the second volume of this series.

Greater meaning

When Israel became a nation in 1948, it established the menorah as its national symbol. Prior to that year the menorah had almost never been employed for common use. And, it had seldom been reproduced as an ornament because the rabbis completely prohibited the reproduction of the temple's sacred articles until the nineteenth century.

But the menorah is so much more than a sacred instrument of light! In spiritual terms, we are the branches of the divine menorah. Just as the separate branches of the original were conduits of the fuel that came from the shamash, at the center, so we are conduits of the power, the light, and the glory that comes from Him when He resides at the center of our lives.

As we live our lives here on Earth, sin and disobedience require God to trim away those areas that prevent His light from shining forth. He is faithful to forgive our sin and separate it from His presence, just as the Israelites deposited the wick trimmings outside the camp.

Removing that sin allows His truth, mind, and spirit to flow through the wick unimpeded, giving forth His light as a witness to all. As our high priest, Yeshua carefully tends His lampstand. Even if our light should grow dim, He will not extinguish a smoldering wick (Matthew 12:20, Isaiah 42:3) but will breathe on it and re-ignite it with the light of His Spirit.

In summary . . .

- God uses what we call "multisensory teaching" in hundreds of ways.
- He divided the Israelite camp into four distinct sections, to mirror the four covenants.
- He Himself provided the only light in the Holy of Holies; the menorah provided the only light in the inner court.
- The menorah is a divine design, serving as both a literal lampstand and a metaphorical "light unto the world."
- The master menorah also serves as the foundational metaphor for the book of Revelation, upon which all its major events can be overlaid.

6

Myth vs. Truth

The main writer/editor of this book is an opera freak. He's also one of our friends, so we say this in the kindest possible way. A little personal dementia can be perfectly normal. And he likes regular music too, so he's not completely around the bend.

But the fact remains that Michael spent a great deal of his idle youth studying voice and collecting recordings. At one time he had a huge collection of LPs. These have since gone to various university libraries, and now he collects CDs.

Most of those CDs are operatic. In fact, he has *all* the operas of some composers and *most* of the operas of several more. Until recently, one of those "I have them all" composers was Richard Wagner; another was Vincenzo Bellini. And if you know anything of opera you'll realize that these two composers are a long way apart on the stylistic scale, but never mind. That's another subject entirely!

However, not long ago, Michael and his wife, Trish, went through a thorough spiritual rejuvenation. God spoke very clearly to them about several aspects of their lives, and they responded by clearing out anything that did not honor Him. This eventually included clearing out their home, too, which meant that various art objects and books had to go. Never mind that some of the books had been passed down from previous generations and had literally never been taken off the shelves and read. God makes certain

125

things very clear, and one of his ironclad principles is that we cannot have a close relationship with Him if we continue to honor or support anything of a satanic or occultic nature.[1] Doing so is a direct defiance – even a repudiation – of His awesome holiness.

What has particular relevance here, from Michael and Trish's experience, is what happened a week or so after they thought the "rooting out" process was complete. Michael began to hear God telling him quite clearly that some of his CDs would also have to go. Specifially, the very operas he'd been more or less saving for his old age, learning a little about them and listening to them once or twice but not seriously studying them because of their sheer complexity in both musical and narrative terms.

We're referring to *The Ring of the Nibelung* by Richard Wagner, which is actually a series of four very long, very intense operas. They amount to one of the opera world's most prized treasures. So what's wrong with them from a spiritual standpoint?

Only this – that every scene in their convoluted plot lines involves, either directly or indirectly, the exaltation of false gods. Specifically, the so-called mythological gods of the ancient world, in their Nordic incarnations.

Where does blasphemy come in?

Now . . . it's possible to argue that listening to music about pagan gods does not constitute blasphemy against the one true God. Believers do it all the time. Indeed, some believers who know this particular music, and also know that Michael threw all fifteen CDs away (we told you they were long operas, averaging almost four hours apiece), think he's a little crazy!

But where do we draw the line? Can the devotion a committed opera lover pours out on his music of choice constitute "worship" of a false god? In Michael's case, he thought so. And likewise, by the way, with an opera called *Norma*, by Bellini. The most beautiful extract from that opera, often considered one of the loveliest soprano arias in the whole genre, is a piece called "Casta diva." But "Casta diva" is the prayer of a Druid priestess to her false god.

Is that something you would share with Yeshua?

We're not suggesting that owning or admiring occultic items is a salvation issue, but certainly it can be a servanthood covenant issue. If we love Him we show it by our respect and obediance. Far better to err on the side of God than to side against Him.

Unfortunately, however, this whole subject remains somewhat of a mystery for modern believers, for we have long since lost any real sense of what can constitute the worship of false gods. In part, this is true because we have literally incorporated pagan influences, pagan references, and even pagan holidays into the very fabrics of our lives. And into our "religious" observances as well.

We've done so for so many generations that we no longer remember where many of our customs came from. What modern believer, for example, realizes that most of our so-called Easter traditions go back to the worship of the fertility goddess, Ashtoreth (also called Ishtar), who was mentioned so often as an abomination to God when the Israelites were subdoing the land of Canaan (Judges 2:13; Judges 10:6; 1 Samuel 7:3; 1 Samuel 7:4; 1 Samuel 12:10; 1 Samuel 31:10; 1 Kings 11:5; 1 Kings 11:33; 2 Kings 23:13)?

Or that Yule logs and Christmas trees, so closely identified with the birth of Yeshua, have pagan (or, at the very least, non-Christian) origins. For example, the original yule log ceremony was a pagan Viking festival celebrating the sun during the winter solstice, which occurred close to the time we celebrate Christmas today.

These are not missteps that can be easily corrected in our complex, tradition-oriented society, and we're not about to suggest any instant remedies. These are matters for God alone to judge. He knows our hearts and our "degrees of innocence," even as He also knows the precise origin of every thought, action, and intention we ever have.

But pausing to think about some of these issues is a good way to get into the right frame of mind for this chapter on mythology. We have already mentioned the concept of counter-covenant, whereby Satan tries to counterfeit every good thing that God introduces into the world. We'll discuss that subject at length in the next chapter, and in far greater detail in our discussion of Revelation in the second volume of this series.

Right now, a good overall understanding of the dynamics of mythology will help lay the groundwork for some of the concepts coming later. It's important to know what Satan has *already done* to introduce false gods into our history, our modern culture, and – to an extent to which most of us barely begin to appreciate – into our daily, personal lives as well.

If you get nothing more from this chapter than a vague awareness of how much our modern culture has been influenced by ancient mythology . . . well, maybe that'll be enough.

Let's begin at the beginning

The English word *myth*, which comes from the Greek word *mythos*, signifying *word* or *story*, has different implications for modern Judeo-Christian believers, anthropologists, folklorists, psychologists, and literary critics. Like poetry, mythology claims to offer a way of understanding the world through metaphor. It celebrates ambiguity and contradiction. Stories adapt and change according to the teller and the context; myths are not fixed and dogmatic but fluid and interpretive.

However, does myth have anything to do with the Bible? Absolutely not! The Bible is a meticulously detailed, historically accurate compilation of prophetically inspired Hebrew writings.

However, the culture that was responsible for protecting and transmitting the oldest foundational texts for a majority of the present-day translations of the Bible (especially of B'rit Hadashah) was primarily a Greek culture. These are the same people who idolized hundreds of false gods, whether created in the imaginations of their own writers or imported from somewhere else. Recall Paul's description of Athens, with false idols and statues of false gods on every corner:

> For as I passed along and carefully observed your
> objects of worship, I came also upon an altar with
> this inscription, To the unknown god. Now what you
> are already worshiping as unknown, this I set forth
> to you (Acts 17:23).

Here in the present age we tend to think that mythology is the study of something that has *always* been a myth – something always known to be mostly untrue. But the people who worshipped the false gods of mythology also sacrificed their children to them! They believed with all their hearts that random fate, manipulated by the whims and passions of their false gods, controlled their destinies. They lived their pitifully constrained lives accordingly, in fact-free zones of fear.

Somewhat later (and at the risk of repeating some of what we mentioned in chapter two), the descendants of these same people also developed a system called Greek hermeneutics (*hier* = system of, *minutiae* = details) to interpret their own mythology. And later, of course, they bequeathed the same methods to us for studying the Bible; that is, Greek methods for studying Hebrew scriptures.

As we have mentioned in chapter 1, they believed that the text "worked" on two levels only, the *literal* and the *allegorical* (spiritual).[2] Beyond that, based on the mythological texts on which they developed their methods, they were also used to assuming that a given text would automatically reflect 75% creative imagination and contain only 25% of truth. As we said earlier, by even the most charitable standards, that built-in presumption would leave a lot of room for them to interject their own biases!

Alfred Edersheim had much to say about this subject; here's just one example:

> In reference to this new Greek allegorical interpre-
> tive method, "any repetition of what had been
> already stated would point to something new. These
> were comparatively sober rules of exegesis, not so
> the license he [Philo] claimed of freely altering the

punctuation of sentences, and his notion that, if one from among several synomymous words was chosen in a passage, this pointed to some special meaning attached to it. Even more extravagant was the idea, that a word which occurred in the Septuagint might be interpreted according to every shade of meaning which it bore in the Greek, and that even another meaning might be given it by slightly altering the letters.[3]

In fact, maybe it's time to be even more blunt. Let's say it categorically – when converted Greek philosophers interpreted the Hebrew Scriptures they used a system of interpretation that was designed for an entirely different purpose. It was woefully inadequate for dealing with God's words, and they got a lot of wrong answers.

Worse, some of those "wrong answers" have subtly contaminated our understanding of certain scriptures for hundreds of years. Thus, thousands of people today read Matthew 5:17 ("Do not think that I came to abolish the Law or the Prophets; I did not come to abolish but to fulfill.") and believe that we're completely freed from observing those nasty, outdated "laws" of the Old Testament because Yeshua came to "fulfill" and thereby cancel the law, rather than coming to "interpret" it as the Scriptures really say.

Indeed, in this particular passage, because we also get the meaning of "law" wrong (Hint: The word translated as "law" is actually "Torah" and refers to all of the Old Testament scriptures, not just to the 10 commandments and the 603 principles for living), we fail to understand that He was *fulfilling prophecies*, not *cancelling divine principles*. His life on Earth was meant to illuminate the Holy Scriptures that had pointed toward Him and promised His coming for centuries. He came, literally, to show us how to live holy lives. In the process He obliterated nothing.

For another example, consider Revelation 16:15:
> "Behold, I am coming like a thief. Blessed is the one
> who stays awake and keeps his clothes, so that he
> will not walk about naked and men will not see his
> shame."

How often have you heard anyone explain that the "naked-ness" this verse refers to has only to do with a lack of physical garments? On the contrary, it has everything to do with the protective *covering* provided to Adam and Eve, representing an eternal *covenant* with the God who created that very concept. But because we depend on Greek translations and Greek insights we miss out on what "naked" really means. We also think that coming "like a thief in the night" refers to some kind of soundless, sly, cat-burglar infiltration. On the contrary, this is a Hebrew idiom meaning that He will come boldly, like an armed intruder who kicks in the door and makes sure everyone in the neighborhood knows he's there (cf, 1 Thessalonians 5:2).

Worse yet, have you ever heard someone say, "This verse has to be understood spiritually, not literally?" That perspective comes from a Greek and not a Hebrew mindset.

Despite all the above, even today the precepts of Greek hermeneutics are staunchly defended by many Bible scholars, despite their origin, their smoothly integrated bias, and their original purpose. And every time we thereby miss the deeper meaning that God intended for us to apprehend, our loss in understanding can be profound.

Hebrew hermaneutics

Conversely, the Hebrew culture and language were (and still are) both markedly different from those of the Greeks. Likewise with their interpretive standards. *Hebrew* hermeneutics is a totally different system of logic, used for thousands of years for close, accurate, highly detailed interpretations of Scripture.

Hebrew hermeneutics requires the interpreter to agree to a rigorous moral standard of unbiased, truthful translation. To the Hebrew mind, Scripture is 100 percent true. That's the starting point. And unlike Greek mythology, Scripture operates on *four* levels simultaneously.

1) *p'shat* = simple, direct
2) *remez* = hinting
3) *darash* = commentary, comparison
4) *sod* = deep, hidden

By way of illustration, let's look through *Hebrew eyes* at a well known passage from the King James translation. Revelation 3:20 says, "Behold, I stand at the door, and knock: if any man hear my voice, and open the door, I will come in to him, and will sup with him, and he with me." How might this passage be viewed at each of the four Hebrew hermeneutics levels?

1) At the most simple and direct *p'shat* level, most everyone gets it. They understand that Yeshua is saying that we need only open our hearts' door for him to come in and bring salvation to our souls.
2) At the hinting (*remez*) level, Yeshua is referring to deeper covenant. It is his desire to begin the family relationship interaction, leading to the betrothal covenant.
3) At the *darash* level, Yeshua partners with us through our acceptance of His sacrifice to purge the evil from our lives.
4) At the *sod* level, Yeshua is not only the Messiah but is also our Groom, coming to offer deliverance through betrothal, the ultimate covenant. And the process begins with opening the door.[4]

Going right back to what we said above, when someone asks whether a particular "meaning" of a particular passage is literal or spiritual, he's asking the wrong question. Truly, it's always both, and more!

Where does that little bit of "truth" come from?

To come back, now, to where we started, the 25 percent of truth found in mythology is made up of common threads that intertwine throughout the separate bodies of myth from all cultures, from almost all of recorded history. Mythology is each society's way of telling stories, mostly untrue but entertaining and even "classic" nonetheless, about its own "unique" religion.

Sadly, to emphasize something we've said before, *mythology was almost never a "myth" to the people who fashioned and revered it.* In every case, once it was created it came to be believed without reservation, often unto senseless death. We need only consider all the human sacrifices made to malevolent, implacable "gods" to weep for such evil-induced ignorance.

But to look again at their beginnings, almost every one of the common threads of truth that wind their way throughout mythology, no matter how cunningly they twist and turn, came straight from the Bible. Unfortunately, mythological stories tend to plagiarize and re-tell biblical stories not as they were given by God but from Satan's perspective instead. In a sense it's "history" as Satan himself would rewrite it, if he could.

For example, most historical myths have a creator-god that made the physical world and then was either destroyed by his creation or faded into the background. In Egyptian mythology the god Ra, "the lord without limit," came into being and created air, water, land, plants, and animals. Eventually, Ra grew so old and feeble that he could not even control his own spittle. His son, Shu, succeeded his senile father, but soon he grew decrepit as well. He then abdicated in favor of his son Geb, who in turn yielded sovereignty to Osiris.[5]

The Greek creator was the Titan Prometheus, fashioning mankind from clay and water. Sound familiar? He was eventually supplanted by Zeus, who then asserted his divine supremacy over man.[6]

The gods demand worship

The creators of mythology commonly morphed the trees, sky, sea, and the elements (fire, air, water, and earth) into gods, gave them imaginary personalities, and convinced others to worship them.

For example, Norsemen worshipped the "world tree," Yggdrasil, who provided protection and nourishment to them and the nine worlds in which they believed. Their "all-father" god, Odin, willingly sacrificed himself on this tree to seize authority and power.[7] The twisted quasi-parallel with the story of Yeshua's own sacrifice on the cross, often called a "tree," is striking.

According to mythology, man's worship of these gods was required. If he ignored them they would not help him when he got into trouble. Worse, the gods would curse him by sending wrath or vengeance. Odysseus angered the Greek sea-god, Poseidon, by not showing him proper homage. The price Odysseus paid for his disrespect was ten years of wandering, a voyage Homer named *The Odyssey*.

Worship often took the form of sacrifices, which included the giving of fruit, animals, money and other valuables, devotion, and often even human children (Leviticus 20:2). The Egyptians sacrificed the Hebrew children to Nun, the fertility goddess of the Nile. Ishtar, the Babylonian earth-goddess, also required child sacrifice to gain her favor.

This same goddess, incidentally, as shown in Table 6-1, is the Ashteroth, or Astartes, of scripture (II Kings 23:13, I Samuel 7:3,4). We derive our modern word "Easter" from Ishtar, one of the biblical variants of the word Ashteroth. Ashteroth was the goddess of love and fortune, the Queen of Heaven. She was also the goddess of fertility.[8] Thus we have our "innocent" Easter symbolism involving bunny rabbits (What's more fertile than a rabbit?), eggs, and baby chicks.

Table 6-1: Devil/God/Goddess Equivalents

Biblical Entity	Biblical gods	Image	Babylonian	Egyptian	Greek	Roman	Norse
Lucifer	Chemosh or Milcom I Kings 11:33	Creator, Son, Morning Star	Marduk Jeremiah 50:2	Ra	Zeus	Jupiter	Odin
Abaddon	Molech Leviticus 18:21	Death	Nergal II Kings 17:30	Osiris	Hades	Pluto	Hela
Jezebel	Ashtoreth or Ishtar I Kings 11:33 Jeremiah 44:17–19	Queen of Heaven	Astarte	Isis	Aphrodite	Venus	Freya
Nephilim	Offspring of angels & women	Hero – Men of Renown	Nimrod and the Golem	Horus	Hercules	Romulus and Remus	Thor

Ishtar, Nun, and other pagan entities were recognized as the gods of *life*, yet required the *destruction* of life to appease them. They also encouraged the use of hallucinogenic drugs, to help the worshipper enter a more receptive state of consciousness.

In many myths, the gods had intercourse with human women and produced demi-gods called *men of renown* or *men of old*, paralleling Genesis 6. The story of Hercules is a classic example, although it is only one of many.

But even though the concept of gods mating with humans came straight from the Bible, it still got horribly twisted. The pagan cultures of Genesis 6 did not recognize the "sons of God" as fallen angels. They viewed them as true gods, as higher beings sent directly from heaven. They were totally unaware that they were actually making sacrifices and offering their women to fallen angels, not to representatives of the true God of the universe. Thus the myths that evolved from that "little bit of truth" were not only hopelessly distorted from the very beginning – *they were also passionately believed.*

Mythology: A daily habit

As fascinating as all this may seem, how does it relate to modern day? Well, for starters, many of our current customs, holidays, and religious systems find their sources in mythology. Likewise with the days of the week, as shown in Table 6-2.

Table 6-2: Days of the Week

Current	Origin	Meaning or Source
Sunday	Sun'sday (Greco-Roman)	Named in honor of the sun
Monday	Moon'sday (Greco-Roman)	Named to worship and honor the moon goddess
Tuesday	Tyr'sday (Norse)	Named for Tyr, the god of war
Wednesday	Wodin'sday (Norse)	Named for Odin, the chief god of the Norse; known to the Greeks as Zeus
Thursday	Thor'sday (Norse)	From Thor, the Norse god of thunder and son of Odin
Friday	Freyaday (Norse)	Goddess of marriage; actually Hera, wife of Zeus
Saturday	Saturnday (Greco-Roman)	Recognizes the Roman god, Saturn

Why are the days of our week named after pagan gods? The people from which the modern English language evolved had deep roots in medieval European culture. These were heavily influenced by the Anglo-Saxons, who descended from the Norse people and their Roman conquerors. Thus, the days of the week are named after a mixture of Nordic and Roman gods.

Although our culture has adopted these pagan names, we do not openly worship the gods they represent. It would be ludicrous to insinuate that anyone today gives credence to Thor or Odin by using their names for the weekdays.

Yet millions of Americans actively pursue the "will of the gods" in several more subtle ways that many of us accept without reservation. For example, did you know that those who read their daily horoscopes are actually paying tribute to a Greek god? The modern horoscope originated as part of the ritual worship at the temple of Apollo.[9] The zodiac has not been altered in twenty-five hundred years, although the courses of the stars certainly have.

How many believers today "innocently" read their horoscopes and perhaps even halfway believe what they read? How many would claim that the whole exercise is simply fun and games? Yet the zodiac dates all the way back to the Babylonian empire. Its influence can be seen in all the major, post-Babylonian kingdoms of the world. For thousands of Babylonians, charting their life by twelve constellations was a primary form of pagan worship, their way of seeking the will of the gods.

Other shadows from other times

Strands from mythology and the bogus "philosophies of the gods" are also prevalent in our modern movies and books. Most of our holidays come from pagan festivals and practices. The planets and constellations, and many of the months, are named after mythological gods as well.

These are basic facts about our own culture, of which we often are sadly ignorant. Our modern society is literally immersed in pagan culture. In that sense, though mythology is clearly a collection of untrue stories about false religious belief systems, many of the untruths those stories teach have not been relegated to the dark closet of man's past. Mythology's sources are ancient but mythology is very much alive and thriving today.

What's really very scary is also equally clear. As recorded in the Bible, the Lord's condemnation of astrology – and any similar manifestations of the "truth perversions" that have been part and parcel of mythology for thousands of years – is absolute and unequivocal. God calls these things divination, or witchcraft, and condemns them as abominations. He says that anyone who practices such forms of worship would be cut off from His people, or worse: "You shall not allow a sorceress to live" (Exodus 22:18).

And yet, at least in the case of astrology, our society finds this not only an acceptable practice but an honored one as well. Indeed – who was that president's wife who invited astrologers into the White House itself and paid them to perform?

The nephilim/mythology connection

What's the bottom line in all this? Well, we know that mythological systems of belief spring from every corner of the world, have many common roots, and tell variations on common stories.

We also know where they get a large share of their raw material. Therefore it's no coincidence that they all tell similar stories of "gods" having sex with human women and producing offspring that become "heroes" and "great men of renown." That's exactly what was recorded in Genesis 6:1–4, and it's repeated innumerable times in mythology. For example:

- Hercules, offspring of Zeus and a human woman
- Perseus, offspring of Zeus and a human woman
- Siegfried, offspring of Wotan (Wodin) and Sieglinde (from Wagner's "Ring")

Sadly, the truth is somewhat different. As we discussed earlier, in the real world, fallen angels had sexual relations with human women and produced hybrid creatures called nephilim. But these offspring were not "great men" in any positive sense. In fact, they were not men at all, and God did not create them!

On the contrary, there's something else going on here, something most believers never think about. Since his days in the Garden of Eden, Satan has never changed. He still aspires to be God. In fact, just before the second coming of the true Messiah he will claim to be the Redeemer and take God's place in His temple (Daniel 9:27). But that's in the future. What happened in the past is equally diabolical.

The common deceptions of mythology are intentional. They represent a relentless, ongoing, multi-thousand-year attempt by Satan and his minions to delude mankind into believing that they, meaning Satan's devils themselves, are divine.

But they are not any more "divine" than any of the fantasy creatures created through mythology. They are no more worthy, no more like the true God of the Universe, than Zeus, Odin, Prometheus, and all the others.

All of these satanic initiatives, these pathetic deceptions, will lead us directly into counter-covenant with the enemy if we do not discern the difference between godly and satanic creations.

Again – let's be clear! The so-called "men of renown" refer-enced in the Bible were actually nephilim. They were evil, despicable creatures whose souls are now demons, just like the ones Yeshua exorcised from the Gadarene madman and sent into the herd of pigs (Matthew 8:28–34). And those from whom the nephilim came, the fallen angels called "teraphim" in the Genesis 6 account, are certainly not gods either. On the contrary, put as plainly as we know how, they are devils.

What makes all this abundantly clear, in addition to many pas-sages from both the Bible and other independent sources, is the book of Enoch. As we have already indicated, in the time of Yeshua, Enoch was part of *Hebrew Scripture*. The rabbis of that era were also more than passingly familiar with it. It is quoted or referred to in II Peter 2:12,13; 3:10; and Jude 14–16. If we'd been there, using the word "Bible" as we do now, Enoch would have been part of "our" Bible.[10] Yeshua Himself memorized it, along with all the rest of the Tanakh and Mishnah, as part of his rabbinical training.

Enoch tells of human women who had sexual relations with fallen angels (teraphim). Chapter seven of Enoch, which we re-printed in chapter four of this book, relates the story in startling detail and explains how these women, who also became seducers of men, were called *sirens* and were judged by God. The Greeks adapted this story and warned their sailors to avoid their own ver-sion of the sirens, who (according to the Greeks) used their voices in song to lead men to their death at sea. In other words, not *all* of that story was fantasy.

A powerful delusion

Again, the net result of all this is that many polytheistic religions, rooted in mythology, have been handed down through the genera-tions and are still with us. Their "sacred stories" attempt to convince mankind that other beings are the real gods, worthy of honor and homage, instead of the God of the Bible.

Sadly, though you might think rational people would know better by now, they keep falling for it! Many put up huge sums of money to explore these ridiculous myths and false religions, often with great fascination and reverence, on the perilous assumption that, even if it's wrong it can't possibly be harmful. Most recently, such ill-considered "re-connections" with ancient myths have spawned everything from a renewed interest in horoscopes to mother-earth (Gaia) worship.

But no matter what our motives might be, most of the seemingly modern "New Age" metaphysical concepts that we now embrace, no matter how "new and original" they seem to be, are still rooted in ancient Greek, Egyptian, and Babylonian religions. And all of these are simply false, even though their own sources – the ancient myths, endlessly reworked – are themselves rooted in some truth. The problem is that Satan always manages to use them to twist and turn people away from the truth.

The net result is clear. The very devils who saw the face of our God and turned away from Him are now the ones doing the "teaching." The adversary had to present man with a form of worship that would still seem palatable, given man's prideful nature. Doesn't Satan always take truth and give it a hidden, perverse twist? We've already talked about how he sometimes comes as an angel of light.

He has consistently offered man a philosophy – or perhaps even a convoluted series of interrelated *philosophies* that were all based on *25% truth and 75% imagination*.

Does that sound familiar?

A great revival?

The church today is predicting a great revival in the near future, with many people being saved just before Yeshua's second coming. There could be some truth to this, but the Bible is silent on any such expectation. The appearance of a "great multitude . . . standing before the throne and in front of the Lamb," in Revelation 7:9, "who have come out of the great tribulation" (Revelation 7:14), must be understood in context.

That vast throng is part of the marriage of the Lamb and His bride, but the assumption that they must all have been "evangelized" by the 144,000 "Jewish witnesses" in the last days is based on other false assumptions and is simply not consistent with the rest of Revelation, as we will explain in much more detail in volume two.

On the other hand, what the Word of God *does* predict, many times with powerful emphasis, is not a coming revival but a great deception and a great falling away. Second Thessalonians tells us that a spirit of delusion will come in the last days, and it will cause many to turn away from the Truth and believe in lies. "For false Christs and false prophets will arise and will show great signs and wonders, so as to mislead, if possible, even the elect" (Matthew 24:24).

One more point. This passage does not mean to say that it's not possible to deceive the elect. A more accurate rendering would suggest that false prophets will arise who will mislead *even those who should know better*. "Some of those who have insight will fall, in order to refine, purge and make them pure until the end time; because it is still to come at the appointed time" (Daniel 11:35).

Finally, the book of Revelation unmasks the greatest counterfeit of all time. Commonly known as "antichrist," a more accurate translation of the Hebrew would be "false messiah." He will attempt to replace God in the hearts and minds of mankind, and for a time he will succeed. But God's guaranteed victory in the end is not a guarantee that we will all, automatically, participate in that victory with Him.

We are instructed to watch and be ready, to make ourselves pure for our Bridegroom (Matthew 24:42, Revelation 19:7). This is a time to review our lives – to identify our foundations, hold to God's values, renew our obligations to Him, and remove any form of worship we offer to the pagan concepts, customs, and practices that have permeated Western thought.

We need to run, not walk – as fast as we can and as far away as we can get – from any devils or demons that masquerade as our great God of the universe. In the words of Paul, "Therefore, my dearly beloved, shun [keep clear away from, avoid by flight if need be] any sort of idolatry [of loving or venerating anything more than God]" (1 Corinthians 10:14, AMP).

On the other hand, if we absolutely cannot run away, as James said, "Submit therefore to God. Resist the devil and he will flee from you" (James 4:7).

In summary . . .

+ All the great myths of the world, no matter how fascinating and even "real" they may seem, are based on a smidgen of truth with a lot of falsehood stirred into the mix.
+ That "smidgen of truth" almost always comes directly from the Holy Scriptures.
+ Invariably, mythology reduces the one true God to a pitiful being (or group of beings) with quasi-human, quasi-God-like characteristics, motives, and abilities.
+ Worse yet, all mythological gods supposedly either share or completely usurp the one true God's unlimited power.
+ Thus they are all pretenders to the throne, just like Satan himself.
+ Which, of course, is no coincidence, for that's who inspired their invention in the first place!

7

Counter-Covenant

For many years, especially in the late 19th and early 20th centuries, respected scientists all over the world talked about the possibility that man would one day discover such paradigm-shifting physical elements as "anti-matter," and such liberating physical forces as "anti-gravity." Well-known authors, including Jules Verne, H.G. Wells, and their modern counterparts, Isaac Asimov and Ray Bradbury, wrote elaborate stories and even entire novels based on such "futuristic possibilities."

Counter-covenant is a term we coined to identify the anti-matter and anti-gravity inventions of Satan. The difference is that Satan's "anti-God" inventions do not represent science fiction. They are entirely real.

They are also entirely derivative, for Satan is a copycat. Except for pure evil itself, nothing unique ever seems to originate with him.

That lack of innovative ability fits his character perfectly. Satan is the ultimate deceiver, who builds his most enduring deceptions by falsifying things that others created first. In fact, that's almost his entire *modus operandi*. Starting with his performance in the Garden of Eden, he's been doing two things extremely well for thousands of years.

First, just as he took on the identity of a serpent, he almost always hides out in someone else's clothing. And second, just as he lied about God's original intent for Adam and Eve, he always twists the words and distorts the deeds of others. He then uses the resulting perversions against us.

When it comes to the sacred covenants God has established with His sons and daughters, Satan rises to new heights of deception. Or to be more accurate, to new lows.

The seven counter-covenants of deception

In a moment we will identify the satanic counter-covenants that exactly and precisely duplicate – in reverse – the patriarchal covenants created by God to heal mankind from his brokenness. God established these seven patriarchal covenants with His own people, from Adam to Yeshua (see chapter two). But before we do that, let's understand one additional thing. It's not enough to know what Satan's counter-covenants are. It's equally important to understand where they fit into the grand scheme for the End Times.

As we explained in chapter five, the fundamental metaphor for the book of Revelation is the menorah. In volume two you will begin to see, in minute detail, how the image of the menorah functions as an overall framework for Revelation. Meanwhile, here in chapter seven we want to offer you a brief preview. It simply isn't productive to talk about God's covenants, versus Satan's counter-covenants, without showing you a little bit of how everything fits together.

As seen on our menorah diagrams that will be part of volume two, Satan's seven counter-covenants take up positions on the left side of the lampstand, while God's occupy the right side. In a moment we'll examine each one of Satan's. But first, let's do some math!

Different kinds of angels

Revelation 12:1–10 explains how one-third of the angels rebelled and were cast out of heaven. Literally, "And his tail swept away a third of the stars of heaven and threw them to the earth" (verse 4). The dragon's tail in question, of course, belonged to Satan.

We also know that there are three kinds of angels: cherubim, seraphim, and teraphim. And, as we indicated in chapter four, we consider it likely that a third of the angels from each of these three angelic orders were cast out with Satan.

Scripture teaches that there are now four cherubim around the throne of God (Ezekiel 1:5–14). If four cherubim remained after one-third had fallen, in the beginning the original number would have been six. We know the names of the four who remain: Michael and Gabriel (Jude 9, Daniel 10:13, Luke 1:19), and Uriel and Raphael (Apocrypha: Esdras 4:1).

So, who were the two who rebelled?

One is the archangel we often know as Lucifer, whom we've elected to call Satan in this book. Scripture identifies him as the covering angel who stood above the throne in the beginning ("the anointed cherub that covers with overshadowing wings"), shining forth his light (Ezekiel 28:11–19). The other cherub was Abaddon, mentioned by name in Job 26:6, Job 28:22, Job 31:12, Psalm 88:11, Proverbs 27:20, and in two more passages:

> Sheol (the place of the dead) and Abaddon (the abyss, the final place of the accuser Satan) are both before the Lord — how much more, then, the hearts of the children of men? (Proverbs 15:11 AMP)

> Over them as king they have the angel of the Abyss (of the bottomless pit). In Hebrew his name is Abaddon [destruction], but in Greek he is called Apollyon [destroyer]. (Revelation 9:11 AMP)

When these two powerful angels fell from grace, their areas of responsibility and influence were immediately altered. No longer was Lucifer/Satan a covering angel, enlightening the pathway of covenant that led to full relationship with God, illuminating and revealing what is true. Instantly he became the fallen angel of darkness, blinding and deceiving, leading people *away* from God and into unholy relationship with himself.

> And the great dragon was thrown down, the serpent of old who is called the devil and Satan, who deceives the whole world; he was thrown down to the earth, and his angels were thrown down with him. (Revelation 12:9)

> So the dragon was enraged with the woman, and went off to make war with the rest of her children, who keep the commandments of God and hold to the testimony of Jesus. (Revelation 12:17)

By the same token, Abaddon, the angel of life, was hideously transformed into the angel of death. Adam and Eve's sin brought about enslavement to the law of death for themselves and for all creation. In the Scriptures, death is repeatedly personified as an actual entity:

> O death, where is your victory? O death, where is your sting? (I Corinthians 15:55)

> I looked, and behold, an ashen horse; and he who sat on it had the name Death. (Revelation 6:8a)

Note, also, that Revelation 9:11, quoted on the previous page, also personifies death.

Abaddon, as Death, was therefore intimitely involved in each of the seven counter-covenants. Whether by Cain's outright act of murder, by which he offered a sacrifice of worship to death, or by Esau's covert desire to hunt down and destroy his brother (Genesis 27:41), both of which we will discuss in a moment, Abaddon is given the worship he craves as Satan's partner. Indeed, in Revelation, chapter 13, Abaddon is the "beast out of the earth."

Satan despises God and desires to possess His authority and power. Since that is impossible, he switches to Door Number Two and desires the identity and authority that God gave mankind. Remember, his own authority has long since been taken away. So, since the moment of his fall, Satan has directed his diabolical efforts at sabotaging God's plan for His children. Those efforts take the form of (1) overt opposition to God's plan and (2) his counterfeit strategy to deceive us into accepting him as lord in place of Yeshua.

Within that context, before we look at specific counter-covenants we need to first understand the nature of "sin" itself.

Three categories of sin

Much has been written about the story of Adam and Eve. One thought that truly encapsulates what happened goes like this: "Man would not have been made in the image of God if he did not possess the faculty to distinguish between good and evil. If he lacked such a capability, his obedience or disobedience would have no moral significance."[1]

By his decision to listen to the deceiver, mankind, God's chosen bride, handed God a divorce. Iniquity was now woven into the fabric of the souls of Adam, Eve, and all their descendants. The decision to determine for themselves what was right and wrong brought a fundamental change in the basic nature of humanity.

Rather than continuing to interact with the supreme God of the Universe via any of the covenant relationships (of which all four would have been appropriate), mankind began to entertain foolish feelings of (or at least desires for) equality.

Here are the three specific Hebrew words that scripture uses to expose the heart of fallen man.

1) *Avon* (ah-**vone**) is the Hebrew word for *iniquity*. Iniquity is *the weakness or tendency to fall under temptation in specific areas*. However, avon is not sin in the generally understood sense. It manifests itself in various ways by bringing thoughts and emotions into our lives that we know are evil. But it does not involve taking action based on those thoughts.

2) *Hatah* (ha-**tah**) is the Hebrew word for *transgression*. Transgression is more than the weakness of iniquity; it is *the action of violating God's principles* and means "to miss the mark." Thus, hatah carries with it the idea of making a mistake, of violating God's principles then picking yourself up, repenting, seeking God, and trying to restore covenant with him.

   In contrast to avon, hatah involves taking action on what we thought or felt; it means violating God's principles. But we still don't identify with it. When we commit a transgression of the hatah type, then correct ourselves and repent, God applauds us. To fight the good fight is honorable.

3) *Peshah* (pe-**shah**) is the Hebrew word for *sin*. It literally means defection or rebellion; to make counter-covenant. Peshah is *deliberate sin, consciously choosing to violate God's principles and identifying with the principles of evil* in a clear act of *rebellion*.

When you are "in peshah" you are no longer struggling against your sin as you do in transgression, or hatah. For example, how many times have you heard someone say, as a justification for their misbehavior, "Hey, that's just who I am; take it or leave it!" That's what God calls rebellion (peshah), and that's what John was referring to when He said, "Be ye therefore perfect, even as your Father which is in heaven is perfect" (Matthew 5:48, KJV). He was saying, "Stop your rebellion against God and his principles."

To put all three together, let's say you have a weakness (avon) for stealing. If you give in to it you add a transgression (hatah), by stealing on purpose. You regret it afterwards and return what you swiped. But beyond that, if you identify with stealing, make no effort to stop, and excuse your behavior by saying that the store has all the money it needs while you have none, you have crossed the line into rebellion, peshah.

To win, to avoid sin entirely, you have to be aware of your weaknesses, recognize temptation when it comes, and turn away. Needless to say, you can't get to number three if you stop at one or two. Unfortunately, all three of these Hebrew words are usually translated into English as the catch-all word, "sin," with no distinctions and no gradations.

By understanding that God began the process of restoration at the very moment of man's fall (i.e., Adam and Eve's avon, hatah, and peshah), we get a clearer picture of God's heart and mind. In that context, casting Adam and Eve out was an act of love and compassion, not of anger and certainly not of hatred. If he'd let them stay and eat the fruit of immortality (tree of life), they would have become immortal and locked themselves into an eternal state of sin.

> Then the LORD God said, "Behold, the man has become like one of Us, knowing good and evil; and now, he might stretch out his hand, and take also from the tree of life, and eat, and live forever." (Genesis 3:22)

It's like blocking a child out of the kitchen so he can't burn his hands on the stove. Thus we see God as the ultimate realist about His bride and her condition, yet He remains determined to win her back. Knowing man's horrific tendency toward disobedience and self-destruction, He remained (and still *remains!*) willing to forgive us and re-establish covenant with us.

Indeed – He is longing to remarry us.

Counter-Covenant #1 – Cain kills Abel

In the progressive and inclusive nature of man's counter-covenants with Satan we see the exact opposite of the kind of godly covenant God desires to establish with us. In its place we see unhealthy, destructive relationships that mock His plan of restoration.

Obviously, Satan's attempt to rob man of his God-given identity and authority did not end after his success with Adam and Eve in the Garden. He now focused his attack on the firstborn son, by appealing to the iniquity that had already become an ingrained part of man's soul.

In the biblical story we see Cain struggling with rage and jealousy for his sibling. In the end, when God told him that sin (i.e., transgression, or hatah[2]) was crouching at his door, Cain's final response was to give in to his anger and murder his brother. Basically, Cain said to God; "Fine! You want a sacrifice? I'll give You one!"

> So it came about in the course of time that Cain brought an offering to the LORD of the fruit of the ground. Abel, on his part also brought of the firstlings of his flock and of their fat portions. And the LORD had regard for Abel and for his offering; but for Cain and for his offering He had no regard. So Cain became very angry and his countenance fell. Then the LORD said to Cain, "Why are you angry? And why has your countenance fallen? If you do well, will not your countenance be lifted up? And if you do not do well, sin is crouching at the door; and its desire is for you, but you must master it." Cain told Abel his brother. And it came about when they were in the field, that Cain rose up against Abel his brother and killed him. (Genesis 4:3–8)

The wording in the Hebrew Scriptures even suggests that Cain killed Abel "in the manner of" a ritual sacrifice (with a knife), rather than with a rock, as some teachers assert. Indeed, no rock is even mentioned. In so doing Cain entered his own blood covenant with death, via the blood of his own brother. He became an eager servant of darkness, a transgressor willing to identify with evil.

Counter-Covenant #2 – Lamech kills a man and a boy

In the sixth generation of the lineage of Cain (seventh from Adam), we are confronted with Lamech, a contemporary of Noah (Genesis 4:18). Noah is a righteous son of covenant, a descendant of the restored lineage through Seth (Genesis 4:25, 26; 5:3–29). But Lamech, by his speech and actions, tells us that he is the unrepentant son of an unrepentant son. In Genesis 4:23–24 Lamech continues the covenant with murder begun by Cain. He chooses to become a deliberate servant of evil, forging a link with Cain's crime by boasting to his wives:

> Adah and Zillah, Hear my voice; you wives of Lamech, listen to what I say; for I have slain a man [merely] for wounding me, and a young man [only] for striking and bruising me. If Cain is avenged sevenfold, truly Lamech [will be avenged] seventy-sevenfold. (Genesis 4:23–24)

We don't know for sure what happened, but obviously Lamech was not seriously wronged. The boy simply bumped him, surely not a crime worth the death penalty. Yet Scripture records a double murder in response. Lamech's blood covenant with death is a perverse mirror image of the covenant of Noah, who obediently offered a proper animal (blood) sacrifice in gratitude for deliverance from the Flood.

These first two counter-covenants, Cain and Lamech, fit into the first level of counter-covenant – the servant level – clearly demonstrating a basic scriptural principle. *You may choose WHOM you will serve but you may NOT choose "none of the above."*

Counter-Covenant #3 – Nimrod builds the tower of Babel

The next level of covenant relationship is friendship. It is typified by salt covenant, sharing food together, and extending friendship through hospitality, as demonstrated by Abraham in Genesis 18:1–5.

Sadly, at roughly the same time, an ominous series of events took place that were almost the exact opposites of what was happening in Abraham's life. In Genesis 10:8–9, Nimrod, King of Babylon, is called a *gibor tzayid l'peni*. These words are often mistranslated as "a mighty hunter before the Lord." But the Hebrew word *gibor* literally means "mighty; a proud, powerful tyrant." *Tzayid* means "a hunter; prey taken in hunting; to decimate; to leave barren;" it's also sometimes used to refer to a *devil*. *L'peni* means "in the face." Thus the three words together mean, "a powerful tyrant devil, in the face of God."

This proud predator is infamous for constructing a temple of habitation for pagan deities, the Tower of Babel in the land of Shinar. The Scriptures imply that Nimrod entered a covenant of friendship with evil entities. The extra-biblical history and mythology of the Babylonian empire sustain these conclusions. Clearly, Nimrod was known among Babylonian mystics as a high sorcerer.

A study of biblical timelines will reveal that Nimrod and Amraphel were one and the same. Nimrod was a contemporary of Abraham. Like Abraham, he had a name change and became known as King Amraphel of Shinar (another name for Babylon), one of the four kings that Abraham defeated in battle (Genesis 14:1). Amraphel's name could mean "he speaks forth darkness." Or, in Hebrew word pictures, "first man of chaos, who can speak with authority," obviously the authority of evil. Nimrod was complely invested in procuring spiritual power and authority through relationships with devils. As Abraham was a friend of God, so Amraphel (Nimrod) was a friend of Satan.

Counter-Covenant #4 – Jacob outsmarts Esau

The fourth counter-covenant was made by Esau, twin brother and counterpart of Jacob. When most biblical scholars speak of Jacob they conjure up a picture of a conniving little wimp, a mama's boy, weaseling the birthright from his brother Esau, Isaac's rightful heir. They see a weakling hiding behind Rebekah's skirts, while Esau swaggers forth as a hairy "man's man." They engender disdain for Jacob and sympathy for Esau, who was cheated out of what was rightfully his.

But if we read the story of these two brothers in the original Hebrew, without any false preconceptions, a very different scenario emerges. The Hebrew text explains that Esau knew the use of traps and snares. Even more ominously, Esau's name translates as "watching to destroy covenant." As with Nimrod, God recognized Esau as a hunter and a "destroyer of life," a *tzayid*. In truth, of the two brothers, *Esau* was the conniver, one who provides for his own comfort, a man of violent acts.

Before the birth of these brothers God clearly told their mother Rebekah that the older, Esau (literally by seconds), would serve the younger, Jacob:

> The Lord said to her, [The founders of] two nations are in your womb, and the separation of two peoples has begun in your body; the one people shall be stronger than the other, and the elder shall serve the younger. (Genesis 25:23, AMP)

This was God's idea, which somehow seems to get lost on the "blame Jacob" commentators. Yet Esau was the conspirator – with the willing help of his father, Isaac, he conspired to have the blessing of the firstborn bestowed upon him in secret, a ritual that should always be witnessed by the entire camp. Jacob intercepted this plan, encouraged by Rebekah who had heard God's prophecy firsthand.

Correctly translated, Jacob's name means "heel catcher." This is a Hebrew idiom describing one who will not allow the enemy to win, one who will never surrender. The correct translation gives us quite a different picture of the man who is usually depicted as sly, scheming, and a physically weak whiney-pants – yet physically able to remove a well cover that usually required three or four men to move it (Genesis 29:10). God unapologetically declares, "Jacob I loved but Esau I hated" (Romans 9:13).

Esau had no real regard for the blessing of the Lord and was willing to sell it cheaply for a bowl of lentil stew. This same stew is one that he himself would have prepared if he'd been willing to assume the normal camp duties of the elder son, rather than disdaining them for his beloved hunting and leaving Jacob to make up for his absence.[3]

This *was* the proper duty of the firstborn son – to maintain the stew and serve the whole camp – to assume the role of the servant (shamash) and truly become the greatest in the kingdom of heaven.

Instead, though it was a sin to be a commerical hunter,[4] Esau had clearly rebelled against God's commandments and the responsibilities that were his by birth. Soon after, when he discovered that Isacc had blessed Jacob instead of himself, Esau sealed his covenant with the enemy by marrying Judith and Basemath, two women of the Hittites, a tribe tainted with nephilim blood (Genesis 26:34–35).

Thus Esau courted evil, entertaining unrighteousness in the same way that Jacob courted God in righteousness. While Jacob fulfilled the responsibilities of the elder son, Esau hunted. And while Jacob eventually married properly, Esau did the exact opposite.

Counter-Covenant #5 – Pharoah and Korah

We now come to the fifth counter-covenant, which begins with the story of Moses. Moses received the promise of sandal covenant, the covenant of inheritance. In Exodus 3:5 God told Moses to remove his sandals because the ground he stood on was holy. Taking off his sandals symbolized removing the old (earthly) inheritance (the inheritance he had as a son of Pharoah) and allowing the Lord to cover him with His new inheritance.

Centuries later, Yeshua referenced exactly the same concept when he told the disciples to remove their sandals and allow Him to wash their feet. They would have no place in His Kingdom if they refused to be served by the ultimate Servant of all (John 13:8).

The sandal covenant involves great significance, which might partially explain why Satan's counter-covenants, beginning here, are often bifurcated, or twofold. Let's take each half separately.

1) In Moses' case, outer (overt) opposition came from Pharaoh. Pharaoh boldly resisted Moses and, ultimately, God. As with the other counter-covenants, this one involved a sacrifice of human blood, from the newborn sons of Israel who were cast into the Nile (Exodus 1:22). Pharoah refused to release God's bride, so God bargained with him through the plagues (see "Cup number two" in chapter 3). The final plague unleashed Abaddon, the angel of death, who slew all the firstborn of those who had not applied the lambs' blood to their doorposts (Exodus 12:23). This forced Pharaoh to release the Israelites, which led to the parting of the Red Sea and the destruction of Pharaoh's army.

2) But it didn't end there. Inner (covert) opposition soon came from among the Israelites themselves, specifically from a false prophet. Korah (whose name meant "bald," or "uncovered" in a culture in which no man could go to God without covering) was a Levite who opposed Moses and questioned his God-ordained authority. Like Satan, Korah

155

attempted to usurp the authority and power bestowed upon Moses and Aaron by the Lord. Korah and those who followed him, and all their households, were swallowed whole and taken alive into hell (Numbers 16:33).

Counter-Covenant #6 – Goliath and Saul

David occupies the sixth position on the right side of the menorah – David, the beloved shepherd-king, warrior-poet, and "apple of God's eye." Despite his sin his life was spared; sincere repentance enabled God to bring Yeshua forth from his lineage. Once again we have a twofold counter-covenant, contrasted with David's inheritance covenant with God.

1) David's external counterpart was the giant Goliath, a nephal from Philistia of the tribe of Anak. This monster epitomized a satanic counter-covenant. First Samuel 17 relates how Goliath opposed the armies of Israel, shouting blasphemies against the Lord. He was a chosen champion of the adversary, a true son of Satan. After David slung a stone that bashed Goliath between the eyes, he took Goliath's own sword and cut off his head. In Hebrew understanding the head symbolizes authority. Thus, David severed the authority of the enemy, once again graphically demonstrating that, if we trust and believe in God, Satan will be defeated. In contrast, we fall under Satan's authority through fear and deceit.

2) As Goliath provided external opposition to David, King Saul provided internal opposition. Saul was chosen by God to bear His covenant, yet he continually mistrusted God and sought the enemy's aid, prevaricating and dissembling (i.e., "wimping out") until the Lord stripped him of kingship and bestowed the anointing and authority on David.

But Saul did not yield his throne quietly. He was tormented by an evil spirit and repeatedly attempted to assassinate David, further evidence of Satan's active enlistment of even God's chosen people to engage in active counter-covenants against God.

In his role as the champion through whom the Philistines hoped to conquer Israel, Goliath represented the hoped-for "inheritance" of the enemy. That he was also a nephal simply makes the whole scenario that much more "Satan-connected." In Saul's case, Satan tried to take someone who was already in God's camp and make them fall, by pulling them backwards. Saul tried to remain as king but without God's authority and blessing; Satan tried to use him to usurp the authority and inheritance of God's chosen people.

Counter-Covenant #7 – the false messiah

This brings us to the final and deepest level of counter-covenant, the bridal relationship. As the false messiah, Satan literally attempts to assume the *shamash* position, rightfully belonging only to Yeshua on the master menorah. He also attempts to install his false bride, the harlot, at his side.

The book of Revelation tells of the false prophet, Abaddon, coming like the prophet Elijah, proclaiming the coming of the false messiah. Satan then physically appears on the earth as the false messiah, claiming to be God Himself, forcing mankind to receive the seal of his counter-covenant, the mark of the beast. He then brings forth his own false bride, those in covenant with him, even as he despises her and eventually kills her (Revelation 17:16).

The false messiah thus becomes a treacherous groom, pouring out the blood of his wretched bride. He expects her to pay the price for him. In contrast, the true Messiah, Yeshua, has already poured out His own blood for His bride, as a true kinsman redeemer.

Whose bride are you?

In the history of mankind, God has initiated seven archetypal covenants. He is offering to restore mankind to a marriage relationship with Himself. But the mending/restoration process cannot be accomplished unilaterally by Him. We must choose to respond positively to His gift of covenant.

Meanwhile, Satan continually attempts to preempt God's offer to build relationship with us. He does this by putting forth unholy alternatives to each of the holy covenants of God. Satan still wishes to *seize from us what he lost* in his fall from heaven. He no longer has God-given identity, purpose, or authority. God was compelled by His own holy nature to turn His face from Satan and strip him of those things. Now Satan seeks to usurp *man's* God-given identity, and the authority that goes with it.

Thus, from the beginning of time, mankind has been tempted with an alternate but deceptive relationship, one that promises to satisfy our fleshly ambitions and lusts but brings us only death. The books of Daniel and Revelation document Satan's final attempt to proclaim himself the Messiah and force all of mankind to worship him as God. He still presumes that the deception and subjugation of mankind will bring him the authority and identity he seeks.

The powerful end-time delusion

The Bible makes it clear that during the time of the end we will see a great falling away from the truth (II Thessalonians 2:3, Matthew 24:5, 24). Many will be deceived and influenced by the miracles and power of the false messiah and his false prophet (II Thessalonians 2:9–12). The deception of the false prophet will be so powerful that he will even be allowed to call down fire from heaven, an act God did not permit the prophets of Baal to achieve when Elijah confronted them (I Kings 18:16–39, Revelation 13:13).

As Satan incarnate, the false messiah will have unsurpassed ability to delude the world. A fatal head wound will be miraculously healed, simulating a false resurrection. With this sign as his calling card, Satan will enter Jerusalem and attempt to take God's place in the rebuilt Temple, defiling the Holy of Holies (II Thessalonians 2:3, 4, Daniel 9:27, Matthew 24:15).

Those who choose not to covenant with God will be deceived into accepting Satan's ultimate counter-covenant, thus becoming his false bride. In the end, Yeshua, as the definitive Power over death and hell, will have complete authority to judge the false messiah and those who have covenanted with him (Revelation 20:1-3).

God foretold in Genesis 3:15 that Satan would receive a wound to the head from Eve's offspring. Yeshua fulfilled this prophesy at His death on the cross. By giving up His life for us, destroying the barrier that Satan brought through sin, Yeshua paid the price for our transgressions, destroying the barrier that sin erects between the Father and Adam's race. Thus Yeshua fulfills the requirements of Torah and the conditions of the ketubah, the marriage contract, establishing the eternal purity of His bride.

In summary . . .

- Satan seldom originates anything himself. He usually tries to fool us by duplicating what God ordains, and tempts us with look-alikes.
- Counter-covenant is the term we coined for the evil covenants with which the adversary tries to "counter" God. For example, Satan formed counter-covenants with Cain, Lamech, Nimrod, Esau, Pharaoh, Korah, Goliath, and Saul. He will also counter-covenant with the false messiah.
- According to Hebrew understanding, "sin" can be differentiated into three progressive levels, interwoven but still distinct.
- Despite Satan's efforts we still have ample opportunity to prepare ourselves for the betrothal covenant with God.
- But, we must be on our guard against major satanic attempts at deception during the End Times.

8

Festivals

Not long ago, in the company of several other people, I watched a movie that won four Academy Awards in the year 2000. One well-known critic[1] had called it "One of the greatest movies ever made." We watched a dubbed English-language version; the original was Chinese in every possible respect.

We did not judge it a horrid movie with no plot and no character development whatsoever. Indeed, it was an interesting combination of fantasy and adventure, devoid of nudity and foul language (at least in the English words). But quite frankly, it arose out of a culture of which most modern Americans have very little understanding, and it referenced and depended on concepts of right and wrong, honor and glory, justice and punishment, with which my small group was simply not familiar.

The result? Perhaps it was a great movie in someone else's language and culture, but in English, to us, in many ways it was utterly inscrutable.

When I think about God's festivals I'm reminded of that experience. God Himself ordained the festivals (also called the feasts) that He wanted us to celebrate. He explained everything more than once, with great care, in the books of Exodus, Leviticus, Numbers, and Deuteronomy. For example, in just one of many references, when he explained what to do for the first Passover, the Lord said:

"Now this day will be a memorial to you, and you shall celebrate it as a feast to the LORD; throughout your generations you are to celebrate it as a permanent ordinance" (Exodus 12:14).

And yet, we have separated ourselves so completely from the culture into which God gave those festivals that we have no understanding whatsoever of what they're all about, or why they were given to us in the first place. They're so foreign to us they've become just as inscrutable as the most remote, non-English culture on the planet.

Most often, if we think about them at all we think of them as Old Testament only. And yet, Yeshua carefully observed (and modeled) all the festivals Himself. All the disciples, the apostles, and the early church did the same. Indeed, no one who studies the scriptures objectively can miss a message so big, so obvious, so clear-cut, so unambiguous. It's impossible to ignore it accidentally; we've had to do it on purpose!

"But God meant that only for the Jews! All that stuff passed away once Messiah came! We're not an agricultural society anymore, so how can we celebrate a harvest? Besides, we like Christmas and Easter better!"

Perhaps you've heard some of these excuses. Maybe you've even made a few of them yourself, in perfect sincerity, based on what you've been taught since you were old enough for your first visit to Sunday School. Nevertheless, not a single holiday that the Christian church observes today is truly a "holy day" in the sense that it was directly ordained by God.

God did not ordain Christmas, nor Easter, nor any of the birthdays of any saints elected by the heirarchy of any church in the world. These are not holy days in any "divine" sense – they are manmade institutions, some aspects of which might have God's blessing but none of which were directly established by Him.

Let us say that again: *Not a single holiday that the Christian church observes today was directly ordained by God.*

Fortunately, God holds us accountable only for what we know, which might be a good reason for some readers to skip this chapter entirely! On the other hand, we're not here to point fingers and pass out blame. It's much more important to go forth from here with a firm understanding of what God actually ordained, why He did it, and what it all means in at least two important respects:

1) First, you really need to understand the basics before you can make up your own mind – not about "What's right for you?" but about what's right from God's perspective. A perspective, by the way, which has *never changed* despite what many in the church of today would have us believe.

2) Second, you need a clear understanding of the festivals to better understand the New Testament and Revelation. And that's where we're headed, starting with the next book. So listen up.

Everything in Scripture is connected

To expand on number two above, perhaps the most important reason for studying the festivals, whether you end up observing them yourself or not, is their "interconnectedness" with the rest of Scripture, both the Tanakh (Old Testament) and B'rit Hadashah (New Testament). For example, in chapter five we examined the menorah's pattern of sevens. God's appointed times, His festivals, are consistent with this pattern and tell us a lot about the mind and heart of God.

Just as the menorah that God instructed the Israelites to build and place in the Inner Court of the Temple had seven lights, God also gave His people (and doesn't that include *all* of His people?) seven feasts to celebrate throughout the year, as a reminder of His character, His commitment, His mercy, His promise, and the relationship He desires to have with us.

God wanted His people to join Him in covenant. By instructing us to observe His celebrations, God intended for us to recall both our commitments to Him and His commitments to us. In that way we would continually renew our efforts to live up to His higher expectations throughout the year.

The seven feasts divide naturally into two groups. We celebrate the four feasts of the first group in the springtime, which the ancient Hebrews called "latter rain." We celebrate the remaining three in the autumn, called "early rain."

The spring feasts begin with *Passover*, the first of the Hebrew Holy Days. The next three, all of which directly relate to Passover, include the feasts of *Unleavened Bread, Firstfruits*, and *Shavuot*, the latter also known as *Pentecost*. According to the Roman calendar, all are usually observed in March, April, May, and sometimes June. On the Hebrew calendar, Passover, Unleavened Bread, and Firstfruits always fall in the first month of the Hebrew religious year (or the seventh month of the civil year), Nisan.[2] Shavuot is always celebrated in the month of Sivan.

The autumn feasts include the Feast of Trumpets (*Rosh HaShanah*), the Day of Atonement (*Yom Kippur*), and the Feast of Tabernacles (*Sukkot*). All are observed during the month of Tishri, which is the seventh month on the Hebrew religious calendar (and the first month of the civil calendar) and usually straddles what our Gregorian calendar calls September and October.

Feast #1 – Passover

Passover, which marks the beginning of the religious (i.e., God's) new year, always takes place on the fourteenth day of Nisan, the first month of the Hebrew calendar, which corresponds to March or April. On this day the Jews remember their deliverance from Egypt.

In the Hebrew language the word for Passover is *Pesach*, which literally means "to pass or jump over." On the original Passover the Lord "passed over" all those who had applied the blood of an unblemished lamb to the doorposts and lintels of their homes. In Hebrew understanding, this corresponded to *tav*, the final letter in the Hebrew alphabet, which was shaped like a cross and literally means "sign of the covenant." This same sign also resembled the two sticks that were placed in the shape of a cross inside the body cavity of the Passover lamb, to keep it open as it was roasted, serving as a graphic illustration of the redemption Yeshua provided for us on the Cross at Calvary.

The Passover was not just for those descended from Abraham, Isaac, and Jacob but was given for the whole assembly of the congregation of Israel. This included Egyptians and people from other nations living in Egypt, who chose to join themselves to God's people. We usually think that the twelve tribes of Israel left Egypt by themselves, but many other Gentile people left with the Israelites and formed a mixed multitude (Exodus 12:38). In Exodus 12:48–49, God makes a provision for conversion:

> But if a stranger sojourns with you, and celebrates the Passover to the LORD, let all his males be circumcised, and then let him come near to celebrate it; and he shall be like a native of the land. But no uncircumcised person may eat of it. The same law shall apply to the native as to the stranger who sojourns among you.

Gentiles can thus be counted among the "children of the promise" according to Romans 9:8: "That is to say, it is not the children of the body [of Abraham] who are made God's children, but it is the offspring to whom the promise applies that shall be counted [as Abraham's true] descendants." (AMP)

Gentiles are thus like wild olive branches grafted in among the natural branches (Romans 11:17). Therefore, should we not also celebrate the Passover as God instructed His people? This feast was so important to God that He commanded the sons of Israel, both natural-born Israelites and engrafted Gentiles, to celebrate this day as a permanent ordinance (Exodus 12:14,49). The children of Israel were to be a model to the nations, so that the Gentiles would recognize the greatness of their Hebrew God. Thus Moses could say:

> See, I have taught you statutes and judgments just as the LORD my God commanded me, that you should do thus in the land where you are entering to possess it. So keep and do them, for that is your

wisdom and your understanding in the sight of the peoples who will hear all these statutes and say, 'Surely this great nation is a wise and understanding people.' For what great nation is there that has a god so near to it as is the LORD our God whenever we call on Him? Or what great nation is there that has statutes and judgments as righteous as this whole law which I am setting before you today? (Deuteronomy 4:5–8)

It's also no accident that God placed the promised land, and thereby the feast keepers, at the very center of the ancient world, a tiny area through which most of the major crossroads of trade were routed. The most important trade routes, from Asia, Europe, and Africa, went directly through Israel, while many of the side routes went through Jerusalem. These include the well-known *Via Mares* and the *King's Highway*.[3]

On the first Passover, just as He did when He sent His Son to die on the cross, God did not require any initial participation on our part, only acceptance and obedience (servanthood). Note, also, the language of Exodus 12:27: "You shall say, 'It is a Passover sacrifice to the LORD who passed over the houses of the sons of Israel in Egypt when He smote the Egyptians, but spared our homes.'" In the original Hebrew text, this verse is in the present tense, reinforcing what the ancient sages taught, that there is only one eternal Passover feast that stretches across thousands of years. Moses sits at the same table with Elijah, Isaiah, David, Solomon, and you.

Yeshua, the disciples, and the Apostle Paul (among others) kept this observance as well, recognizing the redemption God had made for His people. We, too, when we observe this feast, connect and identify with *one eternal deliverance by the hand of God*. We partake of the same table that was provided by God through Yeshua, who became the perfect Passover sacrifice. This is symbolically paralleled by the biblical story of God instructing Abraham to sacrifice his son Isaac (Gen 22:1–13). Abraham did not withhold his son from God, as God did not withhold His Son from us. Neither should we withhold ourselves, or fail to lead our families (and, indeed, all those who look to us for guidance) into submission to God.

Sadly, this symbolism and this reminder are both totally lost on many believers today. We do a great injustice to God when we do not respect and honor Him, even if we act (or fail to act) out of ignorance. Indeed, why on earth do God's people not take every opportunity to please God? Since this is how He says He wants us to honor Him, why not do it?

Feast #2 – Unleavened Bread

The Feast of Unleavened Bread is an eight-day period that begins with Passover. Firstfruits also occurs during the same eight-day "week." These three feasts are grouped together as a unity, an *echad* (Exodus 23:14–19, Exodus 12:15–20). The children of Israel were instructed to lift up raw grain (barley) as a wave offering to the Lord.

The week of Unleavened Bread is the response of a "good and faithful servant." Temporarily, leaven represents sin, or contamination. God wants us to clean out and leave behind the leaven of the iniquity of our past lives, just as the Isaelites left behind the iniquities of Egypt.

On Passover God does it all for us; that is, He provides what we cannot provide for ourselves, salvation. But on Unleavened Bread He asks us to do something for ourselves. He askes us to search out and eliminate any sin that may be lurking in our lives. Thus we prevent any *avon* (iniquity) from proceeding to *hatah* (transgression).

By tradition, the Jews start the day before Passover by going around with candles and looking for leavening of any kind. The process of searchig it out and removing it from their houses models what we should be doing in our lives as well, by providing the appropriate response to God's iniative and looking for sin (weakness). When we seek out and work on areas that are not aligned with God's principles, as detailed in His Word, we fufill our obligations within the service covenant.

Feast #3 – Firstfruits

Firstfruits occurs on the first day following the Sabbath after Passover, which is sometimes Resurrection Sunday (Easter) on our Gregorian calendar. The children of Israel were instructed to offer barley as a wave offering to the Lord.

In the ancient Hebrew language, Egypt is known as *Mitzraim*, "a straight and narrow place; a birth canal." One of Yeshua's references to this is a metaphorical picture of being born again in the Spirit:

> Enter through the narrow gate; for the gate is wide and the way is broad that leads to destruction, and there are many who enter through it. For the gate is small and the way is narrow that leads to life, and there are few who find it. (Matthew 7:13–14)

In Hebrew understanding, on the shore of the Red Sea the waters broke and the people of Israel passed through a birth canal on Firstfruits. Historians maintain that, "On being 'delivered' on the shores of the Sinai, at that exact moment Israel was born as a nation and a free people."[4] This event is a precedent in Hebrew tradition for mikveh, which we have already encountered in chapter three as a ceremonial immersion, in running water, with the candidate bowing forward toward God as the source of living waters.

The festival of Firstfruits is a picture of God befriending the faithful servant by blessing his crops. At Firstfruits, the very first of the harvest was offered unto the Lord, yet man's offering cannot compare to the price paid by the perfect Lamb at his crucifixion, on Passover, approximately 2000 years ago. Yeshua was resurrected from the dead on the feast of Firstfruits (not Easter!), giving us a preview of our own glorious destiny. "Yeshua rose from the dead as the firstfruits of those who are asleep" (I Corinthians 15:20).

The progression of relationships to God in the spring feasts precisely parallels the first two covenants. Passover recalls the shedding of blood to "*kippur*" (cover) sin, and corresponds to the blood sacrifice initiated by God to cover Adam's nakedness (Genesis 3:21). The feast of Unleavened Bread allows God's servants to become partners with Him as we search out and remove all leaven (impurity) from our homes, just as Noah partnered with God in cleansing the earth of its iniquity by building the ark. Firstfruits increases the intimacy of our relationship with God as we enter into the friendship covenant, just as He gave Abraham his new name and unconditional promises.

Feast #4 – Shavuot (Pentecost)

If we position each feast on the menorah, moving from right to left, the fourth feast (*Shavuot* – Pentecost) will occupy the shamash position. In English, *Shavuot* means "weeks" and occurs seven weeks (forty-nine days) after Firstfruits (Leviticus 23:15–17). It is a week (seven) of weeks – a menorah of menorahs. Its English counterpart, Pentecost, means "fifty days" in Greek. (Incidentally, if you count to Shavuot from Firstfruits, you start with Firstfruits itself as day one.) The fiftieth day (Shavuot) is a memorial of the moment when God gave the Torah through Moses (Deuteronomy 4:10–14) and filled the elders with the Holy Spirit, as detailed in Numbers 11:24–30:

> So Moses went out and told the people the words of the LORD. Also, he gathered seventy men of the elders of the people, and stationed them around the tent. Then the LORD came down in the cloud and spoke to him; and He took of the Spirit who was upon him and placed Him upon the seventy elders. And when the Spirit rested upon them, they prophesied. But they did not do it again.
> But two men had remained in the camp; the name of one was Eldad and the name of the other Medad. And the Spirit rested upon them (now they were among those who had been registered, but had not gone out to the tent), and they prophesied in the camp.

So a young man ran and told Moses and said, "Eldad
and Medad are prophesying in the camp." Then
Joshua the son of Nun, the attendant of Moses from
his youth, said, "Moses, my lord, restrain them." But
Moses said to him, "Are you jealous for my sake?
Would that all the LORD'S people were prophets, that
the LORD would put His Spirit upon them!"
Then Moses returned to the camp, both he and the
elders of Israel.

The disciples once came to Yeshua with a similar complaint:

John said to Him, "Teacher, we saw someone casting
out demons in Your name, and we tried to prevent
him because he was not following us." But Jesus said,
"Do not hinder him, for there is no one who will perform a miracle in My name, and be able soon
afterward to speak evil of Me. (Mark 9:38–39)

"The rabbis have taught that liberation from bondage in Egypt
was only the prelude to true freedom; it is not realized until the
former slaves voluntarily take on the liberating responsibility of
Torah. Without this they are still slaves in soul and spirit."[5]

The unleavened bread of the first two feasts is now replaced by
the wheat just harvested, offered up on Shavuot as leavened bread
(Leviticus 23:16). During this time of year the Israelites would harvest the dry fruits or grains from their fields. From this harvest God
instructed them to "bring two loaves made of two-tenths of an ephah
of fine flour, baked with yeast, as a wave offering of firstfruits to the
LORD" (Leviticus 23:17). By contrast to the wave offering of raw
barley on Firstfruits, the bread that's offered on Shavuot includes
leaven, here symbolizing increase, not of sin but of holiness.

Through all these examples it seems clear that taking on the
responsibility of Torah is synonymous with receiving the Spirit of
God – to receiving the anointing of the Holy Spirit and prophesying.

To be a friend of God we must actively participate in the increase (leaven) of His kingdom (Matthew 13:33). We can increase with sin or righteousness, depending on whom we covenant with. The rewards of dying daily to our own evil desires bring an increase in intimacy and productivity, as represented by the leavened bread.

The Shavuot feast is the center of all other feasts, yet involves the least ceremony. It doesn't draw attention to itself but, rather, gives light to all the other feasts just as the shamash kindles the six other lamps. Likewise, our increase in maturity with Him should elevate God only, not us and our achievments.

Feast #5 – Rosh HaShanah (The Days of Awe, or Feast of Trumpets)

A brief interlude now follows, and the year progresses in its ordinary fashion until the time of the trumpets draws near. This is the season during which the ancient Israelites harvested figs, grapes, and other fruit; it is referred to as the "early rain" or "wet harvest." *Rosh HaShanah* (literally "the head of the year") ushers in the civil new year with the sounding of trumpets.

> On the first day of the seventh month [almost October], you shall observe a day of solemn [sabbatical] rest, a memorial day announced by blowing of trumpets, a holy [called] assembly. (Leviticus 23:24 AMP)

In Hebrew, this festival was called *Yom Teruah* or "Day of the Trumpet Blast." While it occupied just one day on the calendar, it occupied a 24–hour time slot within a forty-eight-hour period. No one knew exactly which hour or on which of the two days the trumpet blast, literally the "alarm" trumpet blast (call to war) called *Yom Teruah*, would sound. In Yeshua's time, Rosh HaShanah was known as "The Day and the Hour Which No Man Knows." It is the first of the three fall feasts which, grouped together as a unity, another *echad*, are called "The Days of Awe."

The sound of the shofar (ram's horn trumpet) was considered a "thunder" – a call from God. The high priest alone could determine the exact time to blow the trumpet to begin the civil new year. By viewing the stars the priests determined the exact hour and initiated a signal fire. The fire would be relayed from hill to hill, from the eastern wall of the Temple to the Mediterranean Sea in the west. Thus, another name for the Day of the Trumpet Blast was "The Feast of the Lightning that Shines from East to West."[6]

To be ready to respond immediately to the trumpet call, the Israelites carried a bundle filled with all they needed for the journey to Jerusalem or the local synagogue. When the shofar blast occurred, they traveled without hesitation (Matthew 24:17,18) to the house of worship.

Only males of age, or the chosen representatives of each household or community, were required to go to the Temple. Most women and servants remained home and kept the households running. Ironically, though you couldn't normally tell the difference between sons and servants within a given household during working hours, when the Feast of Trumpets drew near the sons were the ones with their backpacks ready!

When asked what would be the sign of His coming, Yeshua gave seven specific references that any Jew of that day would understand to mean "Feast of Trumpets," as shown in the verses below from the 24th chapter of Matthew, verses 17, 27, 31, 36, 40, 41, and 42.

- **Verse 17** – Whoever is on the housetop must not go down to get the things out that are in his house.
- **Verse 27** – For just as the lightning comes from the east and flashes even to the west, so will the coming of the Son of Man be.
- **Verse 31** – And He will send forth His angels with A GREAT TRUMPET and THEY WILL GATHER TOGETHER His elect from the four winds, from one end of the sky to the other.
- **Verse 36** – But of that day and hour no one knows, not even the angels of heaven, nor the Son, but the Father alone.

- **Verse 40** – Then there will be two men in the field; one will be taken and one will be left.
- **Verse 41** – Two women will be grinding at the mill; one will be taken and one will be left.
- **Verse 42** – "Therefore be on the alert, for you do not know which day your Lord is coming.

Rosh Hashanah is the day on which the ancient Jews were to ask for forgiveness; to examine themselves; to *get their houses in order*. And, if they realized that they'd wronged someone during the previous year, they were to make it right before bringing their offerings.

Feast #6 – Yom Kippur

Ten days after Rosh HaShanah comes *Yom Kippur*, the Day of Atonement. "On exactly the tenth day of this seventh month is the day of atonement; it shall be a holy convocation for you, and you shall humble your souls and present an offering by fire to the LORD" (Leviticus 23:27).

Yom Kippur is the holiest day on the Hebrew calendar, but it is an odd mixture. It is a day of fasting and mourning for sin, yet a day of rejoicing in God's provision of a covering. The Jewish custom of wearing the kippah further represents this concept. We dress entirely in white, not black. Kippur, or "covering," is the word for the mercy seat on the ark of the covenant, where the Shekinah presence of God rested. Those who are humble in spirit, and truly repentant, shall find grace as a covering. Those who are not repentant will find judgment. So it is that we wear white, trusting in God to forgive our sins and to complete the work of purity in us.

The last two feasts work together. Hebrew tradition maintains that we are to examine ourselves for thirty days prior to the Feast of Trumpets. God then inscribes our names in the Book of Life on the Feast of Trumpets. After that we have a "final call" of ten more days in which to ask for forgiveness and make restitution. Whether we heed or ignore the trumpet call, on Yom Kippur, what is written in the Book of Life is sealed.

Meanwhile, we know what we are made of yet we trust our Lord to be merciful. He is, after all, not only Master of all creation, He is our friend and extends to us a hand of adoption on the Day of Atonement.

Thus the inheritance of corruption is set aside and we are given an inheritance of righteousness (sandal covenant). Only two things are required as markers of this righteousness: to try to make restitution for past wrongs (our transgressions and our rebellion) and to determine to do better in the coming year (to fight against our iniquity, or weakness). In Matthew 5:22–26, Yeshua reiterates the Yom Kippur principle of repentance and restitution:

> "But I say to you that everyone who is angry with his brother shall be guilty before the court; and whoever says to his brother, 'You good-for-nothing,' shall be guilty before the supreme court; and whoever says, 'You fool,' shall be guilty enough to go into the fiery hell. Therefore if you are presenting your offering at the altar, and there remember that your brother has something against you, leave your offering there before the altar and go; first be reconciled to your brother, and then come and present your offering. Make friends quickly with your opponent at law while you are with him on the way, so that your opponent may not hand you over to the judge, and the judge to the officer, and you be thrown into prison. Truly I say to you, you will not come out of there until you have paid up the last cent."

Thus we know that words are not enough; we must take action to demonstrate a genuine change of heart. "For just as the body without the spirit is dead, so also faith without works is dead." (James 2:26).

Feast #7 – Sukkot

The seventh and final feast is *Sukkot*, the Feast of Tabernacles, celebrated for eight days. Starting on the fifteenth day of the seventh month, God's people are commanded to build booths to live in for a week (Leviticus 23:33–44). These temporary tabernacles (the actual ancient Hebrew word for "dwell" also means "tabernacle") remind us that the world we live in is a wilderness.

Just as God's people wandered in the wilderness, so do we. Our tabernacle here is temporary, but is still a dwelling for the Spirit of the Living God.

Yeshua came in the flesh to dwell among us (John 1:14). Scholars generally agree that Yeshua's birth occurred during the Feast of Tabernacles. Thus, Yeshua dwelt (tabernacled) with mankind for 33 years.

And, even as Rosh Hashana and Yom Kippur typify sandal covenant, Sukkot, our dwelling with God, is the culmination of all feasts, just as marriage is the culmination of all covenants. So, the correlation is absolute. Sukkot is symbolic of the marriage covenant, and anticipates our eternal dwelling with God.

In summary . . .

God's feasts are consistent with the pattern of the menorah lights and the progression of the covenants. They are road maps showing the way in the wilderness and marking important milestones. We can't learn to negotiate the whole map in a few hours; on the contrary, the feasts teach us that our covenant with God evolves over our entire lives and requires regular renewals of commitment.

The question to the church today is, since the beliefs, promises, and hopes of all believers are so completely expressed in these seven feasts, why are they ignored (and, indeed, sometimes even ridiculed) by so many Christians today?

Truly – if you invalidate the feasts you invalidate the sacrifice of Yeshua, for then His death is no longer a fulfillment of prophecy. Consider the meaning of God's appointed feasts again, in sequence:

- *Passover* represents deliverance by the blood of Yeshua. God purchases His people through blood covenant. This servant (blood) covenant, represented by Adam, is a picture of God beginning the process of delivering fallen man. The sacrifice of the blood covenant provides a covering and offers mankind the opportunity to enter into this relationship through obedience.

- *Unleavened Bread* is a call to mankind to participate in the cleansing of our lives. Sin and iniquity (leaven) contaminate and separate us from God. He desires that we make decisions in our lives to forsake those actions, just as Noah responded to the call to servanthood and participated in God's plan to cleanse the house of mankind from the leaven of iniquity.

- At *Firstfruits* we share with God the produce of our lives through the wave offering. It is a picture of mankind (Abraham) offering back to God what He has been given, through friendship, as symbolized in the salt covenant (Genesis 18:1–8).

- God presented the feast of *Shavuot* as an opportunity to enter into a closer relationship by receiving Torah and by being filled with the Holy Spirit. This results in a changed and circumcised heart – a heart for friendship. Jacob, whose name was changed to Israel, wrestled with God in a face-to-face relationship to receive the blessing that was promised. Covenants of friendship with God involve a change of name, as a sign of how God sees you at that moment and how He intends you to be.

- *Feast of Trumpets* is a time of preparation, a call from God to repent and to war against our sin natures. The ruach (breath, wind, spirit) is symbolically represented by the breath blown through the shofar, an awakening alarm calling us to self-examination and preparation for His return. The sound of the shofar was first heard when Moses led the people out of the camp to meet with God at the foot of Mount Sinai.

- On *Yom Kippur*, or Day of Atonement, we respond to God's call with prayer, fasting, and self-examination (acts of repentance). God now gives us an inheritance of holiness. The covenant of sonship was mirrored by David as he received the throne for an eternal inheritance (Psalm 89:29–37). David had many failings but he always returned to God with acts of repentance, trying to right his wrongs.

- On *Sukkot*, God desires us to enter His dwelling. God has placed our lives in abodes of flesh. This is a time for us to build and enter temporary shelters representing our earthen vessels. We also, prophetically, look forward to our union, in our perfected bodies, with Him. We should be reminded of God's ultimate goal to restore mankind to Himself through the relationship of marriage. By offering the renewed covenant, or B'rit Hadeshah, to mankind (Jeremiah 31:31), Yeshua, Son of the living God, took on the image of man and tabernacled with us on earth. A permanent fulfillment of the promise of this feast is His final coming, when He restores all things and sets up His permanent rule on earth. He comes to our house, the earth, as a groom looking for a bride.

—

9

Color

Throughout history, at various times and in various places, certain colors have been associated with certain activities, certain attitudes, and certain classes of people. Thus to be "true blue" means to be honest, forthright, and faithful; to be "black-hearted" means to be devoid of all goodness, compassion, and morality; to be "of the royal hue" means to be high-born, noble, and fully qualified to wear the rich purples of royalty.

Likewise, envy and jealousy are associated with green; cowardice with yellow; anger with red; and purity with white.

But why? Why should we all agree, over the centuries, on the deeper meanings of various colors? Could it be that God Himself, in his never-ending, multifaceted attempts to link important things together for us in as many ways as possible, used color to suggest some of the original associations that come down to us now as "common knowledge" and folk wisdom?

In chapter two we talked about the four different covenant types presented in the Bible, but toward the end of that chapter we also mentioned two more intertwined aspects of the Lord's master system of symbology – color and light. Recognizing how God has woven color and light into His overall scheme will also help us look below the surface of the words and understand much more of the Bible at a much deeper level – especially concepts of relationship and covenant that God wants to have with us.

The elements of light

If you took high school physics you'll remember that every object on the surface of Earth, during the daytime, is constantly bombarded by light. The light we receive from the sun appears colorless. And yet, we know that the foundation of all light is three primary and three secondary colors. The primary colors are red, yellow, and blue. The secondary colors are orange, green, and purple.

However, the separate colors that make up "white light" are invisible to us, until portions of it are reflected by physical objects. In other words, when you see a "red" apple what you're really seeing is the red light that's reflected by that apple. All the other colors are absorbed. Or, to put it yet another way, though the possibilities for shading and blending are limitless, in the simplest possible terms, an apple appears to be red because it *absorbs* all the colors except the particular shade of red that it *reflects*.

Now . . . the absorption/reflection phenomenon that we've vastly simplified above is actually incredibly complex. Very few of the colors that we see are pure primary or secondary colors. Instead, God has designed a system that allows for vast variation. The huge range of colors we experience is produced by an equally vast range of *combinations* of *reflections* of the basic six colors. And every such combination appears different to our eyes.

So, to review, a red apple reflects mostly red light. The various *shades* of red that differentiate one apple from another are all produced by different combinations of reflected light. In the same way, peaches reflect the particular combination of light that produces their unique colors. A brown dog reflects the particular combination of colors that our eyes see as shades of brown.

What does all this mean? Think back to the images of God we've already encountered. God is light; He is the Light of the World; He said so Himself, over and over again. But He is not just any light; He is the purest white, often described as so intense it would kill us if we were to look at it directly. Recall how God protected Moses when Moses asked to see Him (Exodus 33:18–21). Even so, Moses' face shown so brightly, as a result of just partial exposure to God's glory, that Moses had to wear a veil (Exodus 34:29–33) when he spoke to his own people.

But again, what is important to understand right now is that God uses color symbolically to help us keep things in context – to "see" the relationships He wants us to see. So let's return to the larger picture for a moment, then we'll add some further comments on how the science of light and color supports God's eternal truths.

Colors of the patriarchs

What does color have to do with covenant? Understand that the spectrum of colors (all three primary and all three secondary colors), when re-combined, produces white light.

Recall, also, that each of the first three covenant types – servanthood, friendship, inheritance – is represented by one of the three primary colors, expressed not so much like colored ink on a page but, instead, as light.

Servanthood is represented by red light, the color of blood. Friendship is represented by yellow light, the color of unprocessed salt. Inheritance is represented by blue light, the color of the Hebrew concept of royalty. Adam's, Abraham's, and Moses' covenants were represented by those three primary colors.

The same three colors also come together in other combinations as we progress through the covenants, as shown below in Table 9–1. For example:

Table 9-1: Covenant Colors

Covenant	Type	Initiative	Patriarch	Degree	Color
Servanthood	Blood	Initiated by God	Adam	Primary	Red
Servanthood	Blood	Accepted by God	Noah	Secondary	Orange
Friendship	Salt	Initiated by God	Abraham	Primary	Yellow
Friendship	Salt	Accepted by God	Jacob	Secondary	Green
Inheritance	Sandal	Initiated by God	Moses	Primary	Blue
Inheritance	Sandal	Accepted by God	David	Secondary	Purple
Bridal	All Three Types	Initiated and Accepted by God	Yeshua	Whole Spectrum	White

- The color that symbolized God's relationship with Noah was orange, which is formed by combining red and yellow. Noah began the process of building a relationship with God, following in the footsteps of Adam. When God spoke to Noah he was already walking in servanthood; the Lord simply wanted to see a response in return. Noah sacrificed obediently back to God, and thus began to move to the next level of covenant, friendship.
- The color that symbolized God's relationship with Jacob was green, which is formed by combining yellow and blue. Jacob, like Abraham, was a friend of God, walking in a friendship relationship with Him, but he went one step farther. He wrestled face to face with Him in the ultimate *darash*, responding back to God's offer of increased relationship.
- The color that symbolized God's relationship with David was purple, which is formed by combining blue and red. Moses (blue) was given the responsibility to protect the inheritance of the *developing* nation of Israel. David was chosen by God to inherit the throne and both rule and serve the *established* nation of Israel.

Thus we come full circle as the color of servanthood (red) is combined with the color of sonship (blue). The message is clear – to move into sonship/inheritance covenant you must become the best possible servant. Messiah modeled this very dynamic for His disciples in the thirteenth chapter of John, when he took off his outer garments, fastened a servant's towel around his waist, poured water into a basin, and began to wash their feet. When Peter objected He made Himself very clear: "Unless I wash you, you have no part with (in) Me [you have no share in companionship with Me]" (John 13:8, AMP).

Therefore, in Table 9-1, reflected in the patriarchal covenants, we see an alternating pattern of primary and secondary colors. All the primary colors correspond to the occasions when God *initiated* covenant, showing mankind the pathway to increased intimacy with Him. The secondary colors reflect God's response to us when we choose to walk in more intimate covenant with Him, as exemplified by Noah, Jacob, and David, all of whom clearly made that choice.

Overall, the colors God has assigned to the various levels of covenant graphically illustrate the seamless tapestry He conceived so long ago. If the purpose of covenant is to reveal our ongoing responsibilities once we accept our redemption (and we believe it is), then the corresponding colors, especially when they are combined together, serve as a visual expression of how we actually enter into a deeper relationship with God.

What does all this mean?

Red, yellow, and blue light symbolize the first three covenant types. Combined together into the bridal covenant (and we have already learned that each new covenant extends or "builds onto" the previous ones), the combined colors of covenant produce a pure white light, the color of God. Combining the three covenants into marriage with God produces *completion*, the purity of God Himself expressed in the ultimate relationship between us and Him.

To put it another way, God has proposed a pathway of relationship that He has described as covenant. Each covenant builds on the preceding one; therefore each relationship builds on the previous relationship. We also believe that God has assigned colors to visually represent these levels of relationship. As we choose ever-increasing intimacy with God, we become conduits of His light, thereby reflecting more and more of His divine nature. God's ultimate goal is not for us to remain servants, friends, or sons and daughters, but to become His bride. When you combine the spectrum of covenant color back together again, it forms white light, the color of the bride.

But remember – we all have work to be done once we have been redeemed! And the work we have to do is based on, and modeled by, covenant. In Revelation 19:7–8, the bride who is putting on the white bridal garments is allowed to put them on because she has made herself ready:

> Let us rejoice and shout for joy [exulting and triumphant]! Let us celebrate and ascribe to Him glory and honor, for the marriage of the Lamb [at last] has come, and His bride has prepared herself. [8]She

has been permitted to dress in fine (radiant) linen, dazzling and white—for the fine linen is (signifies, represents) the righteousness (the upright, just, and godly living, deeds, and conduct, and right standing with God) of the saints (God's holy people). (AMP)

God is asking us to prepare ourselves once we've been redeemed, by entering into covenant and walking in increasing intimacy of relationship with Him. The concept of being fully prepared to be His bride is revealed and amplified through the re-combined colors of covenant.

Through the prism gently

One more concept relating to color. It's a well-known scientific fact that when you shine pure white light through a prism you break that white light apart into its separate components. You thereby create the spectrum of color that we know as a rainbow.

The colors of covenant occur in the exact order that colors are refracted in the rainbow. From the "least bent" to the "most bent" colors, you start with red and progress through all the colors of the covenants, in order, ending with purple.[1] Again, the unseen world of light symbolizes the hierarchy of covenant. If you're not willing to bend you can't progress; "dying to self" both requires and allows more bending. Red and orange is refracted (i.e., "bent" to the Father's will) the least. In the same way, a servant is the least in the household and undergoes the least restoration of his nature. Yellow and green are refracted a little more; likewise, we usually require more "bending" before we can be called a friend of God.

The sequence continues with blue and purple, the colors of inheritance. Purple is part of the inheritance covenant, representing royalty, the highest form of sonship or daughtership. And, of course, purple requires the greatest modification, the greatest alteration of our sin natures.

In terms of physical temperature, despite how much it might hurt to touch a red-hot poker, red is actually the coolest, least-efficient color of heat, while blue is the second-hottest, just below white.

That's why the gas company tries to keep your stove adjusted to produce a steady blue flame rather than a sputtering yellow or orange one. It's much hotter and therefore a lot more efficient.

In corresponding "human" terms, servants have a smaller influence, which is reflected in their degree of "heat." As you grow in intimacy with God you learn to handle more responsibility. Eventually you get blue-hot. But again, even as that happens your accountability also becomes greater. Recall what happened to Moses for striking the rock; he was forbidden to enter into the Promised Land, a punishment that might have been excessive except that he was the most responsible, closest-to-God person in the entire nation of Israel.

It also takes more and more heat to purify you and make you more effective. Have you ever asked God why you have to go through so many trials and tribulations? What was His answer? Surely, it wasn't because He hated you and wanted to punish you – God is constantly preparing you to become His bride! He's trying to burn out of you all the brokenness, all the impurities, that stand in the way of greater intimacy with Him.

Healing through His presence

To examine all this from another perspective, anything that's fractured can't reflect light correctly. Try looking through broken glasses (1 Corinthians 13:12). Indeed, we tend to be more like broken coke bottles! But once we've accepted His redemption, our responsibility is to enter into successive covenants with God so that He can bring restoration to us. Basically, we are fractured – body, soul, and spirit. We need to get our areas of iniquity and weakness repaired and restored. We need to get all our cracks and fissures made whole so we can perfectly reflect His divine light.

Just as we've explained previously, an object absorbs all the colors of light except for the one that it's reflecting. In the same way, God is light. We need to absorb the colors of covenant into our broken nature so that one day we can reflect the highest levels of relationship.

In response to our needs, as the healing light of God's covenants begins to flow through us it brings healing to all the broken areas in our own lives. This explains why we say that entering into covenant involves the restoration of our entire being. Someone who doesn't respond to God's leading is refusing to get himself restored through carrying the burdens of covenant. As He said in Matthew 11:30, "For My yoke is easy and My burden is light." But God doesn't remove it all.

At the most basic servant level, in response to our commitment to be His servant, His indwelling brings healing and we begin to reflect red. As we embrace the friendship covenant we begin to reflect yellow. And, as we embrace the inheritance covenant we reflect blue. The ultimate, of course, is to progress to a pure, righteous, fully committed marriage relationship with God in which we reflect His pure white light. *Yeshua also recognizes that white light as the color of His bride.* In other words, a bride is one who has been completely healed through walking out the service, friendship, and sonship/daughtership covenants.

Just as each covenant is supported by the previous covenant – while not abolishing it – so also the progression of colors reflects the same concept. So, when you become a friend you are reflecting a new color, yellow, but you are also still reflecting red. When you become a son or a daughter, like a multifaceted jewel you are reflecting a new color, blue, but you are also still reflecting, red, orange, yellow, and green.

One more observation. In terms of how much light is reflected for each color, the whole process is like a circle. Eventually, you should come back to where you started, for a true son is the servant of all. For example, when something appears red it's reflecting about ten percent of the available light. When it appears yellow it's reflecting about fifty percent of the available light. And when it appears white it's reflecting about eighty-five percent of the available light. Nothing reflects one hundred percent of the light, except God, the source.

But surprisingly, as we intimated above, when you get to blue, which represents the inheritance covenant), the percentage of reflected light drops back down to about ten.[2] So just as Yeshua said, to become a true son of God you must become the servant of all.

What about the nephilim?

The connection between the color concepts we have explored here, and devils, demons, and nephilim, will be explored in greater depth in volume two. Meanwhile, consider one or two "teasers" that might help you begin thinking ahead about certain relationships:

- The number God assigned to Himself is 7, which represents completion.
- The number He assigned to mankind, after man sinned, is 6, which is less than completion. It also represents the day we were created.
- The number that therefore represents the three separate parts of fallen man – his body, his soul, and his spirit – is thus 666, which is the mark of the beast spoken about in the book of Revelation. And remember, for those who take this mark, it represents who they are in covenant with.
- On the other hand, through our marriage with God, He desire to "complete" us, restoring man to his previous state, which would also restore our number back to 7, thus perfecting us and removing any possibility of sin from our eternal existence.
- The color that represents the purity of God is white, created by restoring all the light-based colors of covenant.
- By establishing sinful offspring (Genesis 3:15), Satan is offering covenants of his own, with the same colors as God's. However, because Satan will use mankind in his fallen state (666) to establish his kingdom on earth, the colors that represent Satan's covenants will be soil-based, not light-based.
- Soil-based colors, when mixed together, do not create white but a murky brown-black – the color (via the absence of the purity of light) of sin and death.

What a contrast!

In summary . . .

Romans 1:20 says:

> For since the creation of the world His invisible at-
> tributes, His eternal power and divine nature, have
> been clearly seen, being understood through what
> has been made, so that they are without excuse.

This verse reiterates the important truth we want to communi-
cate in this chapter. In fascinating ways, God has revealed his own
invisible qualities through the associations between the colors of
light and divine covenant. In literal terms that we seldom seem to
understand, His creation reflects the various colors of the spectrum. In eloquent terms beyond our ability to emulate, it all speaks
of His existence, of His love, and of His covenant desires for us.

As we prepare ourselves to be His bride, we take on His color,
white. But only by getting ourselves properly aligned with Him
can we become fully functioning conduits of His Holy Spirit. When
we finally do that we become the best possible representatives of
Him. We also see the deep truths in the True Vine and the Tree of
Life constructs. And we recognize the role we play as the branches
of His menorah, the branches of His vineyard, the conduits of His
Holy Spirit, and both the caretakers and the fruit of His tree. It is a
high calling to be all of these things, but especially to be the light
of the world!

> You are the light of the world. A city set on a hill
> cannot be hidden; nor does anyone light a lamp and
> put it under a basket, but on the lampstand, and it
> gives light to all who are in the house. (Matthew
> 5:14–15)

10

Toward Revelation

More than once we have said that many of the subjects we've introduced in these pages really deserve entire books of their own. Actually, we should probably make that statement even more emphatic. *After all this we've just barely scratched the surface!* As you might have discovered in your own life, the more you study the Word of God, especially through Hebrew eyes, the more God seems to reveal.

As the ancient Hebrew adage says, "When you study the Scriptures you swim in the Sea of Torah." Indeed, now that we're at the end of this first volume, the fundamental, passionate belief that we started with does not seem the least bit overstated: *God is the ultimate source of information.* He is also the *Ultimate Symbologist.* His Great Book is multi-layered and multi-faceted, and practically everything He put into it interacts with the rest of the text in ways that are often overlooked in conventional, non-Hebraic, Greco-Roman methods of biblical exegesis.

To put it another way, God's handiwork is every bit as infinite as He is Himself. Electron microscopes help us see this at the subatomic level, while gigantic telescopes help us see it at the universal level. But only God Himself can help us see it at the biblical level.

Again, as we said way back on the first page of chapter one, God Himself made His own attitude toward all of His creation, including the Holy Scriptures, perfectly clear in Proverbs 25:2: "It is the glory of God to conceal a matter, but the glory of kings is to search out a matter."

Volume two is well underway and will take up exactly where we left off here. In fact, now that we've arrived together at this "jumping off" place, let's look ahead and consider how each of the major subjects of this book will tie in with our examination of the book of Revelation.

- ***Chapter One, Scriptural Background and Integrity.*** In volume two we continue to show how the actual words of Scripture themselves, brought together with the characters, events, and customs they actually refer to, often paint far more dramatic and meaningful pictures than the "sublime mysteries" many scholars put forth instead.
- ***Chapter Two, Covenant.*** In volume two we show how His words, given to us through the Apostle John in Revelation, are infinitely more revealing if you start with a "covenant context."
- ***Chapter Three, Betrothal.*** In volume two we show how a basic familiarity with the ancient Hebrew betrothal metaphor leads to a much clearer understanding of the events of the End Times. Many of those events directly relate to the marriage of Messiah and His bride.
- ***Chapter Four, Devils and Demons.*** In volume two we explain how knowing the difference between devils and demons, where they come from, and what they're likely to do in the years ahead can help believers prepare themselves to deal with them. The same knowledge will also help believers recognize the false messiah, the antichrist, and many of their unholy plans and strategies.

- ***Chapter Five, Menorah.*** In volume two we demonstrate how all the major events of Revelation can be organized and charted on a compound menorah, thereby pulling order and coherence out of what has often seemed like chaos and commotion.
- **Chapter Six, Mythology.** In volume two we show how certain ancient myths still influence our perceptions of the book of Revelation, and still distort our understandings of the message God put there for us to discover.
- **Chapter Seven, Counter-Covenant.** In volume two we graphically demonstrate how Satan's counter-covenants line up directly opposite the original covenants God made with His people. We also show how forming covenants with Satan leads directly to eternal punishment, the precise opposite of the eternal rewards promised by God. Understanding counter-covenant will also help you recognize Satan's poorly hidden agenda, revealed throughout the book of Revelation.
- **Chapter Eight, Festivals.** In volume two we clarify the meaning of many direct scriptural references to the timing and the surrounding events of Messiah's literal return to claim His bride. We also show how the book of Revelation honors the timeline of God's ordained festivals. As with covenant, if you don't know the festivals you won't understand what's happening in Revelation. You have to learn the alphabet before you can read.
- **Chapter Nine, Color.** In volume two we show how God's use of color can help clarify the events of Revelation for us. As the ultimate Master Teacher, He knows exactly how to go about reinforcing what He would have us understand and retain. Also, we will be better able to understand the covenant and counter-covenant relationships that some of the players have with each other, as revealed in the book of Revelation, by knowing the meaning of color.

A stand alone document . . .

Despite the forward-looking focus of this chapter, it's important to remember that this book, by itself, is entirely a stand alone document. And the single most important message we hope it delivers is the concept of covenant by which God defines our relationships to Him and to one another.

Overall, the Western church has done a good job of educating us to the salvation message – the proverbial "ticket into heaven," if you will – and millions of people have either accepted or rejected salvation through the blood of Messiah. But the church has *not* done much to show those who have received salvation what their responsibilities after that act of acceptance might be. In far too many instances, salvation has been taught as a one-time event whereby we receive our ticket and then do pretty much as we want from that point onward.

We're saved! Our sins are forgiven! Therefore we have no further duties, and hardly any further need to interact with God on a daily basis.

Sadly, the church often talks about how the Word of God sets us free. In truth it *does* set us free . . . from the sins of our *past*. But it also brings us into a different kind of accountability, not the involuntary servitude under which we labor when we bind ourselves to alcohol, cocaine, or a lawless lifestyle, but to the "yoke partnering" of reciprocal responsibilities, through covenant.

God has clearly called us to separate ourselves from the world, and separating ourselves from the world means replacing our dependence on our own selves, and our worldly institutions, with dependence on God. It means revamping and replacing many of our attitudes, loyalties, and entertainment choices with a new commitment to the things of God. We see flashes of this understanding when pastors and church leaders talk about receiving the gifts of the Holy Spirit. They refer to it when they talk about moving from "milk to meat," when they speak of what the church often seems to consider, from a Greek perspective, to be the "deeper philosophical truths" of the Bible.

But again, what's so seldom revealed to the average new believer is the clear, simple roadmap that Torah provides us through covenant. Covenant delineates a pathway for us to walk. We all start with redemption (salvation), which leads into a servanthood relationship with God. The servant is not responsible to handle or manage anything at an "administrative" level. He's responsible to get his life in order (to take out the trash!), to bring his worldly appetites under control, to bring his life into alignment with God's commandments, to make himself pleasing to God, and to show himself a good steward.

He then moves forward into the kind of deeper relationships that true friends have, relationships involving increased intimacy, a little more authority and responsibility, but still not the ultimate. A friendship relationship is much different from the next stage of growth, which is sonship or inheritance, leading toward betrothal.

The Lord always moves us ahead

God's method is to slowly and methodically invest us with increasing levels of covenant, with increasing levels of responsibility and authority. He does not give us anything to do for which He hasn't already given us the tools; He does not send us anywhere we haven't been prepared to go.

Now, many people instinctively enter into covenant. These are the new believers whose lives literally change – forever! – on the day they accept salvation. These are the ones who begin reading the Scriptures for themselves, every day, even without study groups to guide and support them. They pray daily and get to know God on a personal basis. Most important of all, these are the ones who literally throw themselves on God's mercy, trusting Him from the very beginning to direct the course of their lives from that moment onward. God becomes not just an adjunct to their existence but its very center. They ask Him to be in charge and He always responds.

By contrast, popular culture often teaches the opposite. Because it lacks (and even disdains) any meaningful understanding of the Hebrew roots that underlie every so-called "Christian" nation, popular culture misrepresents God and His Word. It makes Him an ogre and thereby scares away a lot of potential converts. Or, it makes Him a "divine patsy" (or sugar daddy) with the ability to play nothing more than an advisory role in anyone's life – and then only on the most rare occasions.

With respect to the modern church, despite its good intentions, when it does reach the unsaved it often throws many unprepared and immature believers into situations they're ill-equipped to handle. Many times we see the destroyed lives, littering the pathway. People have guilt trips laid on them because they're not involved in various ministries, or not using their "giftings," or not witnessing enough. And many times they quit before they ever get mature enough to handle responsibility of these kinds.

Ironically, what draws us so irresistibly to Him is knowing who He actually is, in context! *When we understand covenant we gain a divine framework for our relationship with God.* We can literally see ourselves being led, gently and compassionately, into an immensely satisfying, increasingly intimate relationship with Him. And gradually we assume increased responsibility and authority as we take the first steps toward maturity in Him.

To put it another way, when we see a large part of the overall tapestry in advance it makes perfect sense. Thus we completely bypass a lot of the condemnation that comes upon the new believer who has been overladen with "responsibility" for things he's really not even supposed to be dealing with at that point.

This is one of the major goals of this book – to reach out to those who are completely unchurched, or have turned away from the church in frustration. God is no angry tyrant, forever changing the rules and waiting to bash you over the head every time you break one! His nature, His plan, and His goals have not changed since the beginning of time. And He will implement that divine plan in your life if you walk in covenant with Him, one step at a time and throughout eternity, exactly as He planned it.

He does not make mistakes and He does not change His mind along the way.

God is the same yesterday, today, and forever.

A word for the non-believer

In our discussions within this book we've tried to show some of the ways in which mankind has been, or could be, deceived. Any such deception, from God's viewpoint, is all about covenant. It's about service to one master or another; it's about allegiance to Him or allegiance to Satan. Obedience to one or the other is always the first level of covenant.

So, our question is, who are you serving? Who are you in covenant with? You can't sit on the fence; you've already landed on one side or the other. We included chapters on devils, demons, mythology, and devil-directed counter-covenant to reveal the subterfuges of Satan as clearly as we could. Therefore, we all need to review our lives to make sure we're not buying into Satan's deceptions, not setting ourselves up to be further (and perhaps finally) seduced by the coming spirit of delusion that Paul talks about in the second chapter of II Thessalonians:

> The coming [of the lawless one, the antichrist] is through the activity and working of Satan and will be attended by great power and with all sorts of [pretended] miracles and signs and delusive marvels—[all of them] lying wonders— And by unlimited seduction to evil and with all wicked deception for those who are perishing (going to perdition) because they did not welcome the Truth but refused to love it that they might be saved. Therefore God sends upon them a misleading influence, a working of error and a strong delusion to make them believe what is false, in order that all may be judged and condemned who did not believe in [who

refused to adhere to, trust in, and rely on] the Truth,
but [instead] took pleasure in unrighteousness. (II
Thessalonians 2:9–12 AMP)

Essentially, what Paul describes above is Satan's ultimate deception. Satan will present himself as the promised Messiah, but in reality he'll be a walking, talking masquerade. He'll even do signs and wonders and deceive people by the thousands (millions?), but those who have responded to the Holy Spirit, entered into covenant, and aligned themselves with the true God of the Universe will not be fooled.

That, again, is why you have to choose. There is no "none of the above" position; as Yeshua said Himself: "He who is not with Me is against Me; and he who does not gather with Me scatters" (Matthew 12:30).

Satan appears to offer power on the emotional, financial, and spiritual levels; he offers "control" and "authority." That's what seems so seductive, yet it's all smoke and mirrors. Satan is a deceiver from the word go; the things he offers aren't even his to promise! On the other hand, God offers far more than Satan can even imagine. And He delivers on every promise – often many times more than we expect, while Satan simply deceives us over and over.

By the way, Satan will offer a bridal covenant also. He offers his bride a kingdom, but what she actually gets in the end is death. By contrast, the bride of the true Messiah will be given the authority to rule over God's Kingdom, alongside Messiah.

Given all that, if you don't have a covenant relationship with God that fills your heart with assurance, no matter what your circumstances might be, we urge you to turn to Him right now. Focus your heart and your mind on Him, and pray this simple prayer:

Dear Yeshua, I believe that you are the Son of God and the only way to God. I believe that you died on the cross (the sign of the covenant), for my rebellion, and rose again so that I might be washed clean and receive eternal life. I admit that my soul is broken; I acknowledge my iniquity and my transgressions before you and hold nothing back. I turn away from my iniquity, my transgressions, and my rebellion. I accept your sacrifice on my behalf, and I ask you for mercy and forgiveness.

I also ask you to accept me as your servant and bring me into a covenant relationship with You. I ask you to take charge of my life, and I look to you for guidance from this day forward. Make clear a new pathway for my life, and grant me the fortitude and courage to walk it out.

Thank you! Amen.

A final note . . .

To go back to chapter one, whether you have just now prayed the prayer of redemption above or have been a believer for years, just as God gave us a "new" book we know that He will also give you a new one as well. And as with us, it's the same one! The Bible is not shallow. No human mind has ever exhausted every avenue of study that opens up within its covers. It renews itself daily for everyone who opens it with a truly receptive heart.

We hope this book will help you by suggesting important avenues of thought and study for the months and years ahead. To go back to the very first analogy we introduced, shaving any part of the body against the grain allows a cleaner result, with fewer accidents and less bleeding.

But repeated exposure to the cleansing blade also brings constant renewal. The trick is to remain vulnerable and receptive to the truth, willfully exposing ourselves to the demands, however mild or grand, that God will eventually raise you up to meet. God does not want you to remain immature and ignorant (Proverbs, chapters 1 and 2). But, if you grow in covenant at God's pace, accepting every nuance of every new invitation He extends, your strength, your commitment, your faith, and your intimacy with Him will grow automatically. Before long, you'll be walking with

Him at levels of intensity that would have been impossible to sustain just months and years before. And they would *still* be impossible, except that He makes no demands on you that you cannot meet with His help.

Join us for volume two of the *Lost in Translation* series, in which we explore the mysteries of the book of Revelation.

See you there!

Appendix A
Comparisons of Enoch with New Testament Scriptures[1]

Enoch	Text from Enoch	New Testament	Text from New Testament, KJV*
Enoch 64:4	And a voice was heard from heaven	Matthew 3:17	And lo, a voice from heaven, saying
Enoch 6:9	The elect shall possess light, joy, and peace, and they shall inherit the earth.	Matthew 5:5	Blessed are the meek, for they shall inherit the earth.
Enoch 50:2, 4, 5	He shall select the righteous and holy from among them; for the day of their salvation has approached ...and they shall become angels in heaven. Their countenances shall be bright with joy...the earth shall rejoice; and the elect possess it.	Luke 21:28 Matthew 22:30 Matthew 13:43	Your redemption draweth nigh In the resurrection...they are as the angels of God in heaven. Then shall the righteous shine forth as the sun in the kingdom of their Father.
Enoch 93:7	Those, too, who acquire gold and silver, shall justly and suddenly perish. Woe to you who are rich, for in your riches have you trusted; but from your riches you shall be removed.	James 5:1 Luke 6:24	Go to now, ye rich men, weep and howl for your miseries that shall come upon you. Woe unto you that are rich! For ye have received your consolation.
Enoch 96:6, 7, 25	Woe unto you, sinners, who say, 'We are rich, possess wealth, and have acquired everything which we can desire. Now then will we do whatsoever we are disposed to do; for we have amassed silver; our barns are full'...They shall surely die suddenly.	Luke 12:19, 20	Compare the parable of the rich man whose barns were full, and who said to himself, 'Soul, thou has much goods laid up for many years, take thine ease, eat, drink, and be merry.' But God said unto him, 'Thou fool, this night thy soul shall be required of thee.'
Enoch 105:26	And I will place each of them on a throne of glory, of glory peculiarly his own	Matthew 19:28	Ye also shall sit upon twelve thrones, judging the twelve tribes of Israel.
Enoch 62:11	In his judgments he pays no respect to persons.	Romans 2:11	For there is no respect of persons with God.
Enoch 38:2	Where will the habitation of sinners be...who have rejected the Lord of spirits. It would have been better for them, had they never been born.	Matthew 26:24	Woe unto that man through whom the Son of man is betrayed! It would be good for that man if he had not been born.
Enoch 19:2	So that they sacrifice to devils as to Gods.	I Corinthians 10:20	The things which the Gentiles sacrifice, they sacrifice to devils, and not to God.
Enoch 22:10, 12	(The angel Raphael addressing Enoch in the region of the dead) Here their souls are separated...by a chasm.	Luke 16:26	(Abraham addressing the rich man from the region of the blessed) Between us and you there is a great gulf fixed.

Enoch 39:3, 4, 7	A cloud then snatched me up...placing me at the extremity of the heavens. There I saw another vision. I saw the habitations and couches of the saints... with the angels...under the wings of the Lord of spirits. All the holy and the elect sung before him, in appearance like a blaze of fire, their mouths being full of blessings, and their lips glorifying the name of the Lord of spirits.	II Corinthians 12: 1–4 Revelation 19:1	I will come to visions and revelations of the Lord. I knew a man in Christ...caught up to the third heaven...whether in the body or out of the body I cannot tell: God knoweth. How that he was caught up into paradise, and heard unspeakable words, which it is not lawful for a man to utter. I heard a great voice of much people in heaven, saying, Alleluia, salvation, and glory, and honour, and power, unto the Lord our God.
Enoch 46:2	This is the Son of man...who will reveal all the treasures of that which is concealed.	Colossians 2:3	In whom are hid all the treasures of wisdom and knowledge.
Enoch 9:3, 4	Then they said to their Lord, the King: Thou art Lord of lords, God of gods, King of kings. The throne of thy glory is for ever and ever, and for ever and ever is thy name sanctified and glorified. Thou art blessed and glorified. Thou has made all things; thou possessest power over all things; and all things are open and manifest before thee. Thou beholdest all things, and nothing can be concealed from thee.	Revelation 17:14; 19:16 Revelation 4:11 Hebrews 4:13	King of kings, and Lord of lords. Thou art worthy O Lord, to receive glory, and honour, and power; for thou has created all things, and for thy pleasure they are, and were created. Neither is there any creature that is not manifest in his sight; but all things which are naked and opened unto the eyes of him with whom we have to do.
Enoch 24:11, 10	I blessed the Lord of glory, the everlasting King, because He has prepared this tree for the saints, formed it, and declared that he would give it to them....The sweet odour shall enter into their bones; and they shall live a long life on the earth, as thy forefathers have lived; neither in their days shall sorrow, distress, and punishment afflict them.	Revelation 22:2 Revelation 2:7 Revelation 22:14	On either side of the river was a tree of life, which bare twelve manner of fruits, and yielded its fruit every month; and the leaves of the tree were for the healing of the nations. To him that overcometh will I give to eat of the tree of life, which is in the midst of the paradise of God. Blessed are they that do his commandments, that they may have the right to the tree of life.
Enoch 85:2	And behold a single star fell from heaven.	Revelation 9:1	I saw a star fall from heaven unto the earth.

Enoch 10:15, 16	To Michael also, the Lord said, Go and announce his crime to Samyaza and to the others who are with him who have been associated with women....Bind them for seventy generations underneath the earth, even to the day of judgment, and of consummation, until the judgment, which shall last for ever, be completed. Then shall they be taken away into the lowest depths of the fire in torments, and in confinement shall they be shut up for ever.	Jude 6	The angels which kept not their first estate, but left their own habitation, he hath reserved in everlasting chains under darkness, unto the judgment of the great day.
		2 Peter 2:4	God spared not the angels when they sinned, but cast them down to hell, and committed them to pits of darkness, to be reserved unto judgment.
		Revelation 20:10	The devil that deceived them was cast into the lake of fire and brimstone...and shall be tormented day and night for ever.
Enoch 21:56	I beheld columns of fire struggling together to the end of the abyss, and deep was their descent. But neither its measurement nor magnitude was I able to discover...Uriel, one of the holy angels...said, This is the prison of the angels, and here are they kept for ever.	Revelation 20:1-3	And I saw an angel come down from heaven, having the key of the bottomless pit (abyss) and a great chain in his hand. And he laid hold on the devil and...cast him into the bottomless pit, and shut it, and sealed it over him.
Enoch 79	In the days of sinners the years shall be shortened...and every thing done on earth shall be subverted and disappear in its season....In those days the fruits of the earth shall not flourish in their season...heaven shall stand still. The moon shall change its laws, and not be seen at its proper period...and all the classes of the stars shall be shut up against sinners.	Mathew 24:7, 21, 22, 29, 30	There shall be famines and earthquakes in divers places...great tribulation, such as was not since the beginning of the world to this time, no, nor ever shall be. And except those days should be shortened, there should no flesh be saved...immediately after the tribulation of those days, the sun shall be darkened, and the moon shall not give her light, and the stars shall fall from heaven....then shall the tribes of the earth mourn; and they shall see the Son of man coming in the clouds of heaven, with power and great glory.
Enoch 61:9	And trouble shall seize them when they shall behold this Son of woman sitting upon the throne of his glory.		

Enoch 47:3	He sat upon the throne of his glory, while the book of the living was opened in his presence, and while all the powers which were above the heavens stood around and before him.	Revelation 20:11–13, 15	I saw a great white throne, and him that sat on it...and I saw the dead, small and great, standing before the throne; and the books were opened, which is the book of life, and the dead were judged out of those things that were written in the books, according to their works. And the sea gave up the dead which were in it, and death and hell delivered up the dead which were in them....And whosoever was not found written in the book of life was cast into the lake of fire.
Enoch 50	In those days shall the earth deliver up from her womb, and hell deliver up from hers, that which it has received, and destruction shall restore that which it owes. He shall select the righteous and holy from among them.		
Enoch 54	In those days shall the mouth of hell be opened into which they shall be immersed; hell shall destroy and swallow up sinners from the face of the elect.		
Enoch 40:1	After this I beheld thousands of thousands, and ten thousand times ten thousand, and an infinite number of people, standing before the Lord of spirits.	Revelation 5:11	I beheld, and I heard the voice of many angels round about the throne...and the number of them was ten thousand times ten thousand, and thousands of thousands.
Enoch 45:3	In that day shall the Elect One sit upon a throne of glory, and shall choose their conditions and countless habitations.	Matthew 25:31, 32	Then shall he sit upon the throne of his glory; and before him shall be gathered all nations; and he shall separate them one from another.
		John 14:2	In my father's house are many habitations.
Enoch 44:4	In that day I will cause my Elect One to dwell in the midst of them. I will change the face of the heaven: I will bless it, and cause those whom I have chosen to dwell upon it.	Revelation 7:15	He that sitteth on the throne shall dwell among them.
		2 Peter 3:13	Nevertheless, we, according to his promise, look for new heavens and a new earth, wherein dwelleth righteousness.
Enoch 92:117	The former heaven shall depart and pass away, a new heaven shall appear.	Revelation 22:1	I saw a new heaven and a new earth, for the first heaven and the first earth were passed away.

Enoch 61:4–9	The word of his mouth shall destroy all sinners, and all the ungodly who shall perish at his presence…Trouble shall come upon them, as upon a woman in travail. One portion of them shall look upon another; they shall be astonished, and shall abase their countenances; and trouble shall seize them, when they shall behold this Son of woman sitting upon the throne of His glory.	2 Thes. 1:9	Who shall be punished with everlasting destruction from the presence of the Lord, and from the glory of his power.
		1 Thes. 5:3	Then sudden destruction cometh upon them as travail upon a woman with child, and they shall not escape.
		2 Thes. 2:8	That wicked whom the Lord shall consume with the Spirit of his mouth.
		Matthew 25:31	When the Son of man shall come in his glory, then shall he sit upon the throne of his glory.
Enoch 66:5–8	I beheld that valley in which…arose a strong smell of sulphur which became mixed with the waters; and the valley of the angels, who had been guilty of seduction, burned underneath its soil. Through that valley also rivers of fire were flowing, to which the angels shall be condemned, who seduced the inhabitants of the earth.	Matthew 13:42	And shall cast them into a furnace of fire.
		Matthew 25:41	Depart from me, ye cursed, into everlasting fire, prepared for the devil and his angels.
		Revelation 20:10	And the devil that deceived them was cast into the lake of fire and brimstone.
		1 Timothy 4:12	The Spirit saith expressly, that in later times some shall fall away from the faith…through the hypocrisy of men that speak lies.
Enoch 48:1–7	In that place I beheld a fountain of righteousness which never failed, encircled by many springs of wisdom. Of these all the thirsty drank, and were filled with wisdom, having their habitation with the righteous, the elect, and the holy.	John 4:14	But whosoever drinketh of the water that I shall give him shall never thirst; but the water that I shall give him shall be in him a well of water springing up into everlasting life.
		Revelation 21:6	I will give unto him that is athirst of the fountain of the water of life freely.
Enoch 2; 26:2b	Behold, he comes with ten thousands of his saints, to execute judgment upon them, and destroy the wicked, and reprove all the carnal for everything which the sinful and ungodly have done and committed against him…[who utter with their mouths unbecoming language against god, and speak harsh things of his glory]	Jude 14, 15	Enoch also, the seventh from Adam, prophesied of these things, saying, 'Behold, the Lord cometh with ten thousands of his saints, to execute judgment upon all, and to convict all the ungodly of all their ungodly deeds which they have ungodly committed, and of all the hard things which ungodly sinners have spoken against him.'

*Biblical text taken from *The Holy Bible*, King James Version (KJV)

Endnotes

Chapter 1: Scriptural Foundations

1. Alfred Edersheim, *Sketches of Jewish Social Life* (Peabody, MA: Hendrikson Publishers, 1994), p. 263.

2. Ibid., p. 95.

3. Because the Hebrew alphabet (i.e., "alephbet") does not use the same Roman letters that our own English alphabet uses, even the most common Hebrew words, when transliterated into English, can be "correctly" spelled in several ways. Thus "tanakh" can also be spelled "tanach," "tanak," and probably other ways as well. Likewise with names such as "Abaddon" – a quick Google search of the Internet will find this name spelled as "Abbadon" by perfectly reputable sources.

4. Go to www.baonline.org, then click on "Study the Books of the Bible," then "Rev.pdf."

5. Alfred Edersheim, *Life and Times of Jesus the Messiah* (Peabody, MA: Hendrikson Publishers, 1993), p. 38.

6. "Yeshua" is an English transliteration of the Hebrew name of our Savior, whom we commonly know as "Jesus Christ." See the *What's in a name?* section near the end of chapter one for more information.

7. David Biven and Roy Blizzard, Jr., *Understanding the Difficult Words of Jesus* (Shippensburg, PA: Destiny Image Publishers, 1994), p. 4-5.

8. Dr. Daniel ben Gigi said this in a seminar at the Messianic Jewish Northwest Regional Conference in Portland, Oregon, in February 16-19, 2001. Also, Roy Blizzard said much the same thing on page 14 in *Understanding the Difficult Words of Jesus*: "Apart from linguistic and cultural arguments for Semitic origin, it remains an important fact that the poor Greek of the synoptic Gospels is found basically only in literary works that are translations from Semitic origins, such as the Septuagint."

9. See Bibliography at the end of this text for a list of books on this subject.

10. Biven/Blizzard, p. 23-25.

11. Ibid., p. 25.

12. C. H. Kang and Ethel R. Nelson, *The Discovery of Genesis* (St. Louis: Concordia Publishing, 1979), p. ix.

13. Frank Seekins, *Hebrew Word Pictures* (Phoenix, AZ: Living Word Pictures Inc., 1994) p. 1.

14. Ibid., p. 2.

15. Ibid., p. 10–11; also *Gesenius* and *Strongs* (see later references).

16. Gesenius, H. W. F., *Gesenius' Hebrew-Chaldee Lexicon to the Old Testament* (Grand Rapids, MI: Baker Books, 1979), p. 138-139.

17. Ibid., 361-362.

18. This word also means "son of" or "a descendant of." Indeed, it is probably most familiar in the "son of" context.

19. It's good to remember that this passage is referring to the Old Testament, not the New. Much of the New Testament hadn't been written yet, nor had it been canonized. And when it was written it was written in the same general fashion as the oral Torah (*Mishnah*), as commentary on the Torah itself. Yet how many believers today think of the New Testament *only* when they read the passage above?

20. Henry M. Morris, Ph. D., *Many Infallible Proofs* (San Diego, CA: Creation-Life Publishers, 1974) p. 41.

21. Josh McDowell, *More Evidence that Demands a Verdict* (San Bernardino, CA: Campus Crusade for Christ, 1975), p 326. McDowell was quoting Albright from *Recent Discoveries in Bible lands*, 1955, p. 128.

22. All of the Old Testament versions that we have today originate in one of a few ancient scrolls. Almost any Old Testament written in Hebrew is an extremely accurate version of the original. Likewise, any of the standard Interlinear Bibles available today will provide you the Hebrew text, correlated with an English translation.

23. We use a version of the *Salkinson-Ginsburg Hebrew New Testament*, which corresponds to the *Greek Textus Receptus* by The Rev. Dr. Eric S. Gabe (2000), published by The Society for Distributing Hebrew Scriptures in Hitchin, Hertfordshire, England. Unfortunately, though the text is free, it's available *only* to Jews and is not otherwise for sale.

24. For the sake of simplicity, we have used the *New American Standard Bible* for most of the longer quotations in this book.

Chapter 2: Covenant

1. Gesenius, p. 141.

2. James Strong, *The New Strong's Expanded Exhaustive Concordance of the Bible* (Nashville, Thomas Nelson, 2001), Strong's Reference Number 1285.

3. Gesenius, p. 142.

4. Ibid., p. 263; this word also means to "polish a sword" or "to restore."

5. Edersheim, *Life and Times*, p. 36.

6. A. D. Adams, C. H. Irwin, and S. A. Waters, *Gruden's Complete Concordance to the Old and New Testaments* (Grand Rapids, MI: Zondervan/Regency, 1968), p. 60. Salt covenant is also specifically referenced in Leviticus 2:13, Numbers 18:19, and II Chronicles 13:5.

7. On a humorous note, whenever a honeymoon extended through the Sabbath (Shabbat), the bride and groom tied their sandals onto the back of their donkey, thus giving them "movable boundaries" and gently negating the prohibition against journeying "beyond their own boundaries" on Shabbat. Whether God actually smiled at this is unclear, but all we know of His nature suggests that, given the circumstances, He probably did!

Chapter 3: Betrothal

1. Barry and Steffi Rubin, *The Messianic Passover Haggadah* (Baltimore: Messianic Jewish Publishers, 1989), p. 7.
2. Ibid., p. 20.
3. Cf Matthew 9:14–16; 25:1–2; Mark 2:19–20; Luke 5:34–36; John 3:28–30; Revelation 19:7; 21:1–3, 8–10.
4. Wilson, p. 246.
5. Rubin, p. 30.
6. Edersheim, *Sketches*, p. 137. Additional reference can also be found as follows: George Robinson, *Essential Judaism: A Complete Guide to Beliefs, Customs, and Rituals* (New York: Simon & Schuster/ Pocket Books, 2000), p. 160.
7. Does "thirty pieces of silver" sound familiar? It's exactly the fee Judas got for delivering Yeshua into the hands of his executioners. Immediately after the third cup at the Last Supper, Judas ran out and accepted thirty pieces of silver from the Levites, who represented the groom's father. Thus Judas symbolizes an unfaithful bride. The law also requires an unfaithful bride to return the bride price to the father of the groom, often through a representative. But Judas fulfilled this requirement himself when he returned the silver to the Sadducees (Matthew 27:3–5; Zechariah 11:2,13).
8. Barney Kasdan, *God's Appointed Customs* (Baltimore: Lederer Books, 1996), p. 47-70.
9. Gesenius, p. 151.
10. Ibid., p. 420.

Chapter 4: Devils and Demons

1. The book of Enoch is an ancient writing attributed to the Enoch of Genesis 5:22. It was originally included in the Hebrew Bible but was later deleted by the Catholic Church at the Council of Constantinople in AD 553 . Although it is currently considered noncanonical, it was accepted as scripture in Yeshua's time and is heavily quoted in the letters of Jude, II Peter, and the book of Revelation. The book of Enoch also appeared more often then any other book of the Bible among the Dead Sea Scrolls. For a sampling of parallel scriptures (i.e., Enoch vs. The New Testament), see Appendix A of this book.

2. Gesenius, p. 413.
3. Ibid., p. 795-796.
4. Ibid., p. 875.
5. Ibid., p. 625.
6. Many students of the Bible believe that angelic beings can't reproduce. Didn't Yeshua say so Himself, in Matthew 22:30? Not exactly; in context, Yeshua was referring to the state of humanity and angels in heaven. Fallen teraphim, on the other hand, are cited in scripture (and also, of course, in the book of Enoch) as *interbreeding with mankind* on Earth (Genesis 6:1–4, II Pet. 2:4–14, Jude 7). The Bible describes an order of angels that take on human form – those that we sometimes "entertain unawares" (Genesis 18 and 19, Hebrews 13:2).
7. Gesenius, p. 557-558.
8. Johannes Wilbert and Karin Simoneau, *Folk Literature of the Tehuelche Indians* (Los Angeles: UCLA, 1984), p. 104.
9. *The Tanakh, the Holy Scriptures* (New York: Jewish Publication Society, 1988), p. 10.
10. Some commentators believe that verses 11–15 of the 7th chapter of Enoch, reproduced above, are out of sequence here and actually belong between verses 8 and 9 of chapter 8 (also included above or on the following page(s).

Chapter 5: Menorah

1. Consider another ancient enhanced-learning technique. Since long before Yeshua's time, Jewish rabbis have memorized the sacred Scriptures by setting them to music and literally singing the text. Over the centuries a number of different musical styles and pronunciations have evolved (Ashkenazi and Sephardic are but two generalized examples), but all use a common method. Tiny markings, called "trope," are added above and below the text, signifying which melody comes next. A trained cantor reads the trope and sings the melody appropriate to the particular style in which he is singing, in a long, continuous stream of sound.
2. Visualization/Verbalization™ was first implemented in modern times, in an ordered way, by Lindamood-Bell Learning Processes of San Luis Obispo, California, with outstanding results.

3. The expression "sitting shiva" refers to an intense, seven-day mourning period that follows the death of a family member or close friend, and usually begins immediately after the funeral. Mourners do not leave the house, do not cut their hair, do not wear leather shoes, and sit on low stools (or the floor) rather than on comfortable chairs. Friends and relatives visit and often bring food. Most of the time the mourners talk about the deceased. Their goal is to face their loss directly and work through as much of the grief as possible.

4. The reference works listed in the bibliography will provide plenty of additional descriptive information beyond what we can include here. We also invite you to study the book of Exodus yourself, especially the last section beginning with chapter 23.

5. The first layer was a covering of linen; the second was twelve curtains of black goat hair; the third was of ram skins dyed red, and the fourth was of badger skins (i.e., in Hebrew *tahash*, in English the *dugong*, a species of seal).

6. The Ark contained the two tables of stone, the pot of manna, and the rod of Aaron that budded and produced almonds, following the Korah affair (Numbers 17:8).

7. Mitch and Vhaza glaser, *The Fall Feasts of Israel*, (Chicago: Moody Press, 1987), p. 84.

8. Estimates for the actual weight of the menorah range from less than seventy to more than ninety pounds. Assuming the higher weight, at $320 an ounce that means the raw material alone was worth almost half-a-million modern dollars. At $400 an ounce (probably a more realistic price) its melt value alone would approach $600,000. The artistic, cultural, and historical value of the finished piece cannot possibly be calculated, but never mind. The one that was in the temple in AD 70 hasn't been seen since Vespasian destroyed the temple and hauled it away. And we have no way of knowing whether that was the actual original. All we know for sure is that the Vespasian/Titus Arch, still standing in Rome and built by the father to celebrate the deeds of his soon-to-be-emperor son, shows a menorah being carried off to Rome.

Chapter 6: Myths vs. Truth

1. God's clear prohibition against practicing divination or sorcery, or engaging in any activities or harboring any items of an occultic nature, is clearly conveyed in Leviticus 19:26, Deuteronomy 18:18, 1 Samuel 15:23, and many other scriptures.
2. Edersheim, *Life and Times*, p. 28-29.
3. Ibid., p. 29.
4. Ibid., p. 14.
5. Neil Philip, *Myths and Legends* (New York: DK Publishing, Inc., 1999).
6. In a not-so-subtle "reverse" twist, the implications of the typical mythology pattern (of the younger god replacing the older one) have subtly influenced Christian thought. Case in point: A crotchety, white-bearded Yahweh, given to fits of destructive wrath, is replaced by his mild and more tolerant son, Yeshua. Yahweh required obedience while Yeshua offers grace. Thus many believers say, "We're not under law anymore." Of course, what they're really saying is quite different: "We don't serve the God of the Old Testament – we serve the God of the New Testament." As far-fetched as it might sound, this image has crept into the minds of many believers even though it's not only blasphemous but polytheistic as well.
7. Philip, p. 71.
8. Gesenius, p. 661.
9. http://www.wikipedia.org/w/wiki.phtml?search=zodiac&go=Go.
10. To see how closely much of the text of Enoch corresponds to the King James Version of our Bible, check out Appendix A at the end of this book.

Chapter 7: Counter-Covenant

1. J. H. Hertz, *Soncino Chumash* (London: Soncino Press, 1962) p. 10.
2. Gesenius, p. 271.

3. As a firstborn son within the ancient Hebrew society, Esau had certain duties to uphold, of which keeping the camp stew was just one. Jacob is typically derided for "hanging around the camp like a momma's boy" when, in reality, he was actually assuming the duties of the firstborn because of Esau's neglect.

4. "As a pastoral people the Hebrews did little hunting as a sport; and their rules of eating preventing their doing so except for food, after the law was given." Alexander Cruden, *Cruden's Complete Concordance to the Old and New Testaments* (Grand Rapids, MI: Zondervan Publishing, 1968) p. 223.

Chapter 8: Festivals

1. Joel Siegel, "Good Morning America," as quoted on the commercial package of the VHS-movie itself.

2. The "modern" month of Nisan was called *Abib* in ancient Hebrew times.

3. Yohanan Ahoroni, *The MacMillan Bible Atlas* (New York: MacMillan Publishing Co, 1963), p. 16.

4. Hayim HaLevi Donin, *To Be a Jew* (New York: Harper Collins, 1972), p. 218.

5. Nathan Ansubel, *Book of Jewish Knowledge* (New York: Crown Publisher, 1964) p. 397.

6. Jacob Neusner, *The Mishnah: A New Translation* (New Haven, CT: Yale University Press, 1988), p. 301-307.

Chapter 9, Color

1. *The World Book Encyclopedia, Volume 12* (Chicago: Field Enterprises Educational Corp., 1967), p. 249.

2. Ibid, p. 253.

Appendix A

1. Richard Laurence, *The Book of Enoch the Prophet* (Kempton, IL: Adventures Unlimited Press, 2000) p. xxv–xxxiii.

Bibliography

Aharoni, Yohanan. (1962). *The Land of the Bible.* Philadelphia, PA: Westminster Press.

Aharoni, Yohanan & Avi-Yonah, Michael. (1968). *The MacMillan Bible Atlas.* New York, NY: MacMillan Publishing.

Backhouse, Robert. (1996). *The Kregel Pictorial Guide to The Temple.* Grand Rapids, MI: Kregel Publications.

Biven, David & Blizzard, Roy, Jr. (2001). *Understanding the Difficult Words of Jesus,* Shippensburg, PA: Destiny Image.

Black, Naomi (Ed.). (1989). *Celebration: The Book of Jewish Festivals,* Middle Village, NY: Jonathan David Publications, Inc.

Brown, William. (1996). *The Tabernacle, Its Priests and Its Service.* Peabody, MA: Hendrickson Publishers.

Byers, Marvin. (2000). *The Mystery: A Lost Key,* Hebron Press, Miami, FL.

Church, J. R. & Stearman, Gary. (1993). *The Mystery of the Menorah.* Oklahoma City, OK: Prophecy Publications.

Cohen, Abraham A. (1995). *Everyman's Talmud: The Major Teachings of the Rabbinic Sages,* Schocken Books, New York, NY.

Cohen, Shaye J. D. (1987). *From the Maccabees to the Mishnah.* Philadelphia, PA: The Westminster Press.

Crossan, John D. & Reed, Jonathan L. (2001). *Excavating Jesus.* New York, NY: Harper.

Donin, Rabbi Hayim Halevy. (1982). *To Be a Jew*. New York, NY: Basic Books, A Member of the Perseus Books Group.

Donin, Rabbi Hayim Halevy, (2001). *To Pray as a Jew: A Guide to the Prayer Book and Synagogue Service*, New York, NY: Basic Books.

Dunn, James D. G. (1992). *Jews and Christians, the Parting of the Ways*. Grand Rapids, MI: Wm. B. Eerdmans Publishing Co.

Edersheim, Alfred. (2000). *The Life and Times of Jesus the Messiah*. Peabody, MA: Hendrickson Publishers, Inc.

Edersheim, Alfred. (1994). *Sketches of Jewish Social Life*. Peabody, MA: Hendrickson Publishers, Inc.

Edersheim, Alfred. (1994). *The Temple: Its Ministry and Services*. Peabody, MA: Hendrickson Publishers, Inc.

Finto, Don. (2001). *Your People Shall Be My People*. Ventura, CA: Regal Books, A Division of Gospel Light.

Friedman, David. (2001). *They Loved the Torah*. Baltimore, MD: Lederer Books.

Frydland, Rachmiel. (1991). *What Rabbis Know About the Messiah*. Columbus, OH: Messianic Literature Outreach.

Frymer-Kensky, Tikva; Novak, David; Ochs, Peter; Sandmel, David F.; & Signer, Michael A. (2000). *Christianity in Jewish Terms*. Boulder, CO: Westview Press.

Gesenius, H. W. F. (1979). *Gesenius' Hebrew-Chaldee Lexicon to the Old Testament*. Grand Rapids, MI: Baker Book House.

Howard, Kevin, and Rosenthal, Marvin. (1997). *The Feasts of the Lord*. Orlando, FL: Zion's Hope, Inc., Thomas Nelson.

Kasdan, Barney. (1993). *God's Appointed Times: A Practical Guide for Understanding and Celebrating the Biblical Holidays*. Baltimore, MD: Messianic Jewish Publishers.

Kenyon, E.W. (1981). *Blood Covenant*. Lynnwood, WA: Kenyon's Gospel Publishing Society.

Kohlenberger, John R, III. (1979). *The Interlinear NIV Hebrew English Old Testament*. Grand Rapids, MI: Zondervan Publishing.

Lamm, Maurice. (1980). *Jewish Way in Love and Marriage*. Middle Village, New York, NY: Jonathan David Publishers, Inc.

Lash, Jamie. (1997). *The Ancient Jewish Wedding . . . and the Return of Messiah for His Bride.* Ft. Lauderdale, FL: Jewish Jewels.

Lattimore, Richard. (1991). *The Odyssey of Homer.* New York, NY: HarperCollins.

Laurence, Richard. (2000). *The Book of Enoch the Prophet.* Kempton, IL: Adventures Unlimited Press (original edition, 1883).

Levy, David M. (1993). *The Tabernacle: Shadows of the Messiah.* Bellmawr, N J: The Friends of Israel Gospel Ministry, Inc.

Martin, Richard P. (1991). *Bulfinch's Mythology: The Age of the Fable, The Age of Chivalry, Legends of Charlemagne.* New York, NY: HarperCollins.

Mason, Steve. (1992). *Josephus and the New Testament.* Peabody, MA: Hendrickson Publishers.

Murray, Andrew. (2001). *The Two Covenants.* Fort Washington, PA: CSC Publications.

Nanos, Mark D. (1996). *The Mystery of Romans.* Indianapolis, MN: Augsburg Fortress.

Nanos, Mark D. (2002). *The Irony of Galatians.* Indianapolis, MN: Fortress Press.

Neusner, Jacob. (1988). *The Mishnah: A New Translation.* New Haven, CT: Yale University Press.

Olitzky, Rabbi Kerry M. & Judson, Rabbi Daniel (Editors). (2002). *The Rituals & Practices of a Jewish Life.* Woodstock, VT: Jewish Lights Publishing.

Philips, Neil. (1999). *Myths & Legends: The World's Most Enduring Myths and Legends Explored and Explained.* New York, NY: DK Publishing.

Richmond, Barbara. (1996). *Jewish Insights into the New Testament.* Woodland Park, CO: For Your Glory, Inc.

Robinson, George. (2000). *Essential Judaism: A Complete Guide to Beliefs, Customs, and Rituals.* New York, NY: Simon and Schuster.

Rosen, Ceil & Rosen, Moishe. *Christ in the Passover.* Chicago, IL: Moody Press.

Scott, Bruce. (1997). *The Feasts of Israel.* Friends of Israel Gospel Ministry.

Seekins, Frank T. (1994). *Hebrew Word Pictures.* Phoenix, AZ: Living Word Pictures, Inc.

Shanks, Hershel. (1992). *Understanding the Dead Sea Scrolls.* New York, NY: Random House.

Stern, David H. (1990). *Restoring the Jewishness of the Gospel.* Clarksville, MD: Jewish New Testament Publications, Inc.

Trumbull, H. Clay (1975). *The Blood Covenant.* Kirkwood, MO: Impact Christian Books.

Trumbull, H. Clay. (1975). *The Salt Covenant.* Kirkwood, MO: Impact Christian Books.

Trumbull, H. Clay. (1975). *The Threshold Covenant.* Kirkwood, MO: Impact Christian Books.

Vernes, Geza. (1992). *The Religion of Jesus the Jew.* Minneapolis, MN: Fortress Press.

Wilson, Marvin R. (1989). *Our Father Abraham.* Grand Rapids, MI: Wm. B. Eerdmans Publishing Co.

Winkler, Gershon. (1998). *The Way of the Boundary Crosser: Introduction to Jewish Flexidoxy.* North Vale, NJ: Jason Aronson, Inc.

Young, Brad H. (1998). *The Parables.* Peabody, MA: Hendrickson Publishers.

LaVergne, TN USA
18 November 2010
205261LV00007B/109/A

9 781589 301993